A Journey Through the Old Testament

The Bible Reading Fellowship

BRF encourages regular, informed Bible reading as a
means of renewal in churches.

BRF publishes three series of regular Bible Reading
Notes: *New Daylight*, *Guidelines* and *First Light*.

BRF publishes a wide range of materials for individual
and group study. These include resources for Advent,
Lent, Confirmation and the Decade of Evangelism.

Write or call now for a full list of publications:

The Bible Reading Fellowship
Peter's Way
Sandy Lane West
Oxford
OX4 5HG
Tel: 0865 748227

The Bible Reading Fellowship is a Registered Charity

A JOURNEY THROUGH THE OLD TESTAMENT

JOYCE PEEL

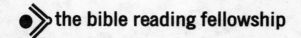
the bible reading fellowship

Text copyright © 1993 Joyce Peel

Published by
The Bible Reading Fellowship
Peter's Way
Sandy Lane West
Oxford
OX4 5HG
ISBN 0 7459 2592 8
Albatross Books Pty Ltd
PO Box 320
Sutherland
NSW 2232
Australia
ISBN 0 7324 0767 2

First edition 1993

A catalogue record for this book is available
from the British Library

Printed and bound in Great Britain
by Cox and Wyman Ltd, Reading

Acknowledgments

I am deeply grateful to the Rev. Cecil Hargreaves, an old family friend, who was at one time on the staff of Bishop's College, Calcutta, and later of the United Theological College, Bangalore, and who was CMS Asia Secretary for eight years. He very kindly read my manuscript and sent me several pages of very helpful and detailed comment, appreciation, criticism and suggestion. I have used almost all of this in revising the text. He also encouraged me to seek publication and pointed me in the direction of the BRF.

I am also grateful to Mrs Florence Shaw who typed my manuscript with such care—correcting my numerous spelling mistakes.

Lastly, a big thank you to Kate and many other friends who have supported me with their encouragement and prayer.

for Kate and others like her

Contents

Introduction

Don't miss this. It's important!

Kate sparked off the writing of this book. So, if you don't like it, blame her. We set off together on a journey of exploration into the Old Testament. Some journeys are boring, but not this one. Kate not only caught my excitement, but fired me up to put pen to paper in order to invite others to join the trail.

My own excitement with the Old Testament started a long way back. It began when, as a student at Oxford, I attended a series of gripping Bible studies on Amos and Hosea, given by Joe Fison, then Curate of St Aldate's, later Bishop of Salisbury. I was so excited that I spent at least half of the money given me for my twenty-first birthday (the other half going on gramophone records) on buying commentaries and other books on the Bible, Old Testament as well as New. I then embarked on what became a lifetime's study on my own.

Later, as a C.M.S. missionary, and drama adviser to the Diocese of Madras, I wrote an epic drama, showing the whole of the Old Testament as one great story. The different playlets within it were acted by different villages and Church institutions, just as the medieval guilds acted the mystery cycles. The epic took eleven hours, covering two nights to act, and was watched by an audience of 5,000!

The reader will therefore understand both my excitement and appreciation of the drama of the Old Testament.

After retirement I joined a Bible study group, where leadership revolved, and everyone prepared a contribution on an agreed subject. The study rightly concentrated on the Gospels and other New Testament books, but, when I eventually suggested we took a look at the Old Testament, I met with some negative reactions.

Muriel, a woman of my own age, had, since being widowed, been drawn to prayer. She believed in learning through experience, and reacted strongly against anything smacking of the intellectual. She had been excited by the Book of Acts, but, when it came to the Old Testament, she said repeatedly that she didn't want to know. It was full of battles and gory deeds. God always seemed to be angry, and threatening to punish people. Anyhow, it was a Jewish book. Why should Christians bother with it? The Psalms of course were an exception.

Kate was different. A young mother, recently converted, she had an enquiring mind, and was eager to learn. But she too found the Old Testament boring, and difficult to understand. Though saying little, she pondered and questioned. Questions of scientific truth and historical likelihood, as well as ethical problems, created barriers for her. She did not see it as being relevant to her own needs. She knew of my own excitement and, when I tentatively offered to teach her, she jumped at the opportunity.

Thus began an exiting adventure for both of us. I began by giving her reasons why I thought a study of the Old Testament was important. What most convinced her was the discovery of what it meant to Jesus, and how it all related to him.

There is a picture, supposedly a photograph, of footprints in the snow. They look like a meaningless collection of smudges on a white sheet. But, if you go on looking at it, suddenly you see the face of Jesus looking out at you. Once seen, you'll always see him there.

The Old Testament is a bit like that. The black smudges are the different problems already referred to. Jesus himself said that the Scriptures—for him the Old Testament—pointed to himself (John 5:39). After his resurrection, as he walked along the road to Emmaus with the two sad disciples, he explained how this was so. They certainly didn't find his Bible study boring!

From childhood, Jesus' mind and spirit were steeped in the Scriptures, its teaching and imagery. His apt questions show that he knew a lot of it by heart. He lived in obedience to the Law of Moses, though he interpreted it according to its spirit rather than its letter. He claimed that he had come, not to abolish, but to fulfil it (Matthew 5:17–20).

How did Jesus come to discover his vocation, and learn what it meant to be the Messiah? It could only have been by a prayerful study of the Scriptures. No one but he linked the Messiah with the sacrificial lamb of the Passover and covenant, or with the suffering servant of Isaiah 53. According to the Gospels, Jesus, in the wilderness, rejected the devil's more attractive scenarios by quoting Scripture and, in the synagogue at Nazareth, he outlined his own programme by reading from Isaiah 61 (Luke 4:16–21). He fulfilled all the prophecies made about himself, some by carefully-planned intention (Zechariah 9:9). As he hung dying on the cross he was reciting Psalm 22. Its opening verse expressed his cry of desolation. Its final verses rang out in his great cry of assurance of hope and fulfilment.

It really isn't possible to understand the deep implications of Jesus' words and deeds without entering into his mental and spiritual world, by studying the Old Testament. How, for instance, can we properly interpret those memorable words 'This is my blood of the New Covenant, shed for the remission of sins', without knowing the part played by the sacrificial lamb in the first Passover and covenant, and the understanding of blood sacrifice to the Jews of his time? To our culture it is alien, distasteful and, therefore, misunderstood.

Another argument for studying the Old Testament came from William Neil's *One Volume Bible Commentary*, incidentally a very good buy. In his first chapter he points out that the whole Bible is one great drama in three acts. Its theme is God's purpose of salvation. It starts with a prologue, Genesis 1–11, which explains why such a purpose was necessary. Act One, the rest of the Old Testament, shows how it began to be worked out in the Jews. Act Two, the Gospels, tells how it was fulfilled by Christ, while Act Three, the Book of Acts and the Epistles, show how it was worked out in and through the Church. The Book of Revelation forms an epilogue, with a series of visions, showing how God's purpose will be brought to its final conclusion.

A drama is difficult to follow if you arrive late, and miss the first act. You don't understand the characters and their interrelationships. You miss the references and clues given to the situation by past events. All good playwrights know the dictum, 'The end lies in the beginning', and the importance of foreshadowing. The patient development of God's purpose, from the beginning to its end, needs to be seen if its wonder is to be fully appreciated. It is on this we need to keep our eye as we study the Old Testament.

A third argument is the relevance of the Old Testament to us as Christians today. All of us, who have put our faith in Jesus Christ, are descendants of Abraham (Galatians 3:29). We are the New Israel (1 Peter 2:9). So, the Old Testament is not just a Jewish book, not even just Jesus' book. It is our book, in which we see our own story unfolding, and leading us to God.

As Kate and I progressed in our exploration, we both began to wish that others too could share in our excitement. So this book came to be written with people like Kate and Muriel in mind. I have tried to preserve the unstuffy approach and raciness of style, but I have submitted the result to vetting by a theological college lecturer, so that glaring omissions and errors, both in approach and detail, could be ironed out. Muriel also consented to read it and said she enjoyed it!

The book is not a substitute for reading the Old Testament. Its object is to act as a key to unlock this Aladdin's cave of spiritual treasure, and help its readers to do their own exploring. That is why some of the references given are deliberately used to arouse curiosity.

Some people may find the constant looking up of references an interruption. It may be best to read the chapter right through, and then, after reading the Bible portions given, go back and look them up.

The Psalms, which are the one part of the Old Testament with which most people are familiar, are discussed only in Chapter 15, but some of them are used throughout as commentary, and more are suggested for further reading, together with parts of the New Testament. The questions provided aim to provoke further relating of the subject matter to our own life and experience.

Finally, a word about the usefulness of different versions and translations, for most of the Old Testament was originally written in Hebrew, though a few of the later books were written in Greek.

Lying around in many homes, too often tucked away, dusty and unread, can be found copies of the King James Authorized Version. Its majestic and resonant prose is unrivalled, and is marvellous for great poetic passages like the first chapter of Genesis and the Psalms. It is profound, and it rings bells in our ears with a familiar sound. This can be a drawback. It can lull us to sleep instead of stabbing us awake. Its main problem is, that like Shakespeare—probably a contemporary of the authors—its language is archaic and obscure.

The Revised Standard Version has ironed out the archaisms, and changed words which have altered their meaning, such as 'prevent' which used to mean 'go before'. Compare the two versions in Psalm 88:13, where the earlier version now makes nonsense. The RSV is also based on older, and therefore more accurate texts, later discovered. It is a version authorized for use by Roman Catholics, Anglicans, Russian Orthodox and other denominations, and so is ecumenical.

For narrative portions modern translations are better. With the discovery of still more ancient manuscripts, they are likely to be even closer to the original. Discoveries, such as that of the Dead Sea Scrolls, have also helped translators to understand the background and meaning of the words used. These new translations, using contemporary speech, make a more lively and instant appeal. The Good News Bible, with its graphic and amusing illustrations, is especially delightful. Even the Laws of Leviticus become less formidable, and make interesting reading. Proverbs become spicy, and so does Ecclesiastes. Its final description of approaching old age and death is particularly vivid.

For the Prophets I personally prefer the Jerusalem Bible. This preserves the poetry with greater beauty and depth. The short lines, and crisp, incisive language, give forcefulness and bite.

The Living Bible is a popular paraphrase. It can help to make both narrative and teaching alive and understandable. But it is important to remember that it is a paraphrase, not a translation, and that a paraphrase is apt to reflect the views of its author. It is best used as an additional aid, and not as a substitute for a translation.

A continuous flow of new discoveries has led to an increasing number of new translations. The New Revised Standard Version (NRSV) has removed unnecessary sexist language, and has included the books of the Apocrypha. Like the New Jerusalem Bible (NJB), the NRSV includes maps and a chronology. The NJB also gives a glossary explaining the biblical meaning of special words.

So, dear reader, having got yourself suitably equipped with at least one Bible, and this book as a guide, set forth on your own adventure of discovery.

1

The Prologue

Genesis 1–11

What a lot we clever twentieth-century people know! From the movement of the galaxies, down to the energies that make up the atom, science has made the most fantastic discoveries. We are deluged with information, and, in the TV programme 'Mastermind', we marvel at those whose minds are crammed with facts.

But what is the meaning of it all? What is life for? Is there any point in it all? These are the questions people are asking today with increasing desperation.

The Bible is not concerned with the whats, wheres and hows of life, so much as with the whys. Genesis means beginnings. It is a book that contains the beginnings of everything significant to the quest for meaning, which the rest of the Bible develops.

Appropriately it begins with a great prose poem on creation, which is best read in the incomparable English of the Authorized Version.

The creation   Genesis 1:1–23

The curtain rises on a dark stage—darkness and void. Gradually we become aware of deep rolling waters, formless, chaotic, yet pregnant with possibility. Look.

Look harder, and listen to the wind: the breath of God. Then perhaps you can see the Spirit of God, like a dove, moving over the face of the waters, or, as Gerald Manley Hopkins puts it:

> *… the Holy Ghost over the bent*
> *World broods with warm breast, and with ah! bright wings.*

Paint the scene with words, colours or music. Here is the essence of drama—contrast, conflict, and suspense. Something momentous is about to happen.

God speaks his Word—the Word by which all things were made (John 1:3–4). And there is light, the light of meaning and purpose. Darkness and chaos are overcome, as by the beam of a lighthouse. 'The light shines in darkness, and the darkness has not overcome it.' Out of that meaning and purpose life is created.

The order in which creation takes place is unimportant. The writer used the cosmology of his day. Nor is the time scale important. 'With the Lord one day is as a thousand years' (2 Peter 3:8). The days of the week have been chosen by the writer as a framework for his narrative. What is all-important is his interpretation.

'It was good.' 'It was good,' and, after the creation of human beings had completed it, 'Behold it was very good.'

The repetition is emphatic. Earthquakes and volcanoes, yes, and scorpions and rats, all are good, and have their place in the intricate design, as ecologists are slowly discovering. But essentially this is not a scientific statement. It is a declaration of faith based on a belief in the nature of God.

Another astonishing declaration of faith is that God made man and woman in his own image. We say of someone, 'he is the image of his father,' meaning we can see his father in him. We are created to be people in whom God can be recognized! True of Jesus, it is potentially true of us all (Colossians 1:15–16). In some people it is easy to see. In others we need to look for it in faith.

In this passage we see a foreshadowing of the Trinity at work. God the Father creates the world through his Son, his Word which gives light, breathed into creation by the Spirit. God's oneness is complex, a network of dynamic loving relationships. We too are complex creatures, striving for a similar loving unity within ourselves, as well as with others, all to be folded into the unity of God (John 17:20–23).

Because of our privileged status, dominion is given us over the rest of creation. Where the image is marred, the privilege is abused.

The final statement of faith is that on the seventh day God rested, blessing it as a day of rest for others. The author, with his deep regard for the sabbath, probably chose the days of the week as his framework with this in mind.

We are not bound by the legal requirements of the Jewish sabbath, but, in our busy stressful world where tension causes so many break-downs, to see God not just as active creator, but being at rest, is of enormous importance. Being is more important than doing. Creative action springs out of stillness and rest (Hebrews 4:9–10). St Augustine wrote, 'Thou hast made us for Thyself, and our hearts are restless until we find our rest in Thee.' Jesus always rested in God, but he still kept times of quiet withdrawal.

'Holiday' means 'holy day' or 'whole-making day'. Recreation is for re-creation.

This first chapter of Genesis is so packed with relevant purpose that it will take a long time to explore and absorb!

For further reading

Psalms 8; 148; the Benedicite (BCP/'A Song of Creation', ASB page 53/ Song of the Three 35–68/Daniel 3:57–90 JB)

Five great myths   *Genesis 2:4—11:9*

'If God made the world good, how come evil has made such a mess of it?' Another familiar and most reasonable question.

No rational or pat answer can satisfy. The Bible deals with the problem in five stories, or myths. We sometimes say, 'Oh, that's a myth' meaning it isn't true, or it's non-existent like some mythical monster. But the word has a more positive meaning. Myths are stories giving answers to questions about the origins and meaning of life, and the relationship between gods and men and women. All primitive peoples have them and the Nordic and Greek myths are familiar to us. What make the biblical myths special are the depth and universality of their truth. Like Jesus' parables, they convey truth with vivid simplicity that can germinate in the mind and heart.

The myth of the creation of man   Genesis 2:4–25

This is a much earlier and more primitive account of creation than that of Genesis 1, but the truths it conveys are just as important. It is much more concerned with relationships. God is seen as a potter, lovingly moulding man out of the earth. Dust we are, and to dust we return! But we are more than dust. God breathes into us the breath of life. This word breath, in Hebrew, is the same as that for wind and spirit. Our spirit is that portion of us which can respond to God's Spirit, and enable us to have a personal relationship with our creator.

Nature is a garden for man to tend. Animals are brought for him to name, as companions and helpers. But man is still lonely, so Eve is created out of one of his ribs.

The whole myth is a profound statement about the relationship between the sexes. Men and women are incomplete without each other. The purpose of marriage is not just sensual enjoyment, or the begetting and rearing of children, it is a sacrament of lifelong union for loving companionship and mutual support.

Two trees of great significance stand in the garden. One is the tree of life, later to be seen growing in the city of God (Revelation 22:2). The other is the tree of the knowledge of good and evil. Eden's happy innocence depends upon its fruit being left untouched. With the art of a great dramatist the author foreshadows the calamity to come, and ends leaving us in suspense.

For further reading

Psalm 128; Matthew 19:3–9; Ephesians 5:22–23

The myth of the Fall   Genesis 3

We don't know when humankind first developed a sense of moral responsibility and guilt. We ourselves don't remember when and how we became aware of them. This story points to our experience of temptation and its consequences.

First comes doubt. 'Hath God said?' Evil appears in an attractive guise. We know something is wrong but we want to do it. So we rationalize and accuse our conscience of just imagining that God is saying 'No'. Then comes the half-truth, 'Ye shall not surely die.' Physical life may continue, but the spirit sickens (Romans 6:23). Next God is portrayed as a jealous tyrant, hostile to our claim to equality. That is what we really want: to 'be as gods'. 'I am the master of my fate:/I am the captain of my soul.' The words express the pride, self-confidence and rebellion of an adolescent!

The choice is made. Man and woman know better than God what is good for them. The fruit is eaten and shared. The immediate consequence is guilt. Fearing the nakedness of exposure they hide. God is not longer thought of as a friend but as a cop!

But there is no hiding from God.

'Adam … Where art thou?'

Where are we in our relationship to God?

Adam is all excuses. He blames Eve. She blames the serpent. Their relationship with each other is now shattered. Forgiveness is only possible when we take responsibility for our faults.

The broken relationship with God leads to the end of a harmonious relationship with nature and the animal kingdom. Man's labour changes from joy to drudgery. The broken relationship between man and his wife result in the woman's subjection. There remains the problem of the tempter. Why a serpent? In the ancient world the serpent was, among other things, a symbol of earthly wisdom and, as such, was—and, in many places, is still—worshipped as a god. This earth wisdom, raised up as a rival force to God—as it is being consciously raised today in 'New Age' cults—is cursed.

A remarkable prophecy is made. The woman's son shall crush the serpent's head, and the serpent shall bruise his heel. This was fulfilled when Jesus, son of Mary, herself daughter of Eve, was nailed to another tree, which became for us the tree of life.

Finally, Adam and Eve are driven from the garden, and the tree of life is guarded by an angel with a flaming sword. So long as these relationships remain broken no paradise can be found on earth. Utopias men and women try to create end up more like hell. Our mortality saves us from catastrophe. How could we bear it if our lives in this state were everlasting? In Jesus our relationship with God and with each other find healing. In him we find eternal life of a different quality altogether, and the gates of paradise lie open.

For further reading

Romans 5:14–15; 8:19–22; 1 Corinthians 15:22–45

The myth of Cain and Abel   Genesis 4:1–15

Sin leads to sinning.

The Greek word for sin means literally missing the mark. An inherent pride and disobedience urges us to go our own way, and, in doing so, we lose our direction and God's purpose for our lives. We are lost. We are in a state of separation from God. He either seems non-existent or like a brick wall! The technical term for this universal situation is original sin.

It does not necessarily imply bad behaviour. We are all by nature sinners, but some of us lead very upright and moral lives. The trouble is that this is apt to make us complacent and censorious of others—like the Pharisees!

But sin does breed sinfulness. Parents who lead blameless lives are sometimes horrified by the wicked deeds of their children. How can such things come about? As with HIV, once immunity is lost Aids can develop. One of the easiest sins to develop in a home is jealousy.

To the Jew who wrote this story the ideal life was that of a shepherd. David was a shepherd, and Jesus called himself the good shepherd who gave his life for his sheep. Tilling the ground was associated with Canaanite Baal worship. This may account for the work allotted to the two brothers. But the reason for God's rejection of Cain's offering was not his occupation but his sin of jealousy. Jealousy leads to hatred and hatred to murder (Mark 7:21).

God questions Cain, 'Where is thy brother?'

Cain, like Adam, rejects responsibility.

'Am I my brother's keeper?'

That question echoes down our history, calling into question all our political, social and economic as well as our personal responsibility.

Are the rich and the comfortably-off to be held responsible for the homeless and hungry? Is the genocide of Jews and Kurds our concern? The consequence of murder is more than broken relationships. It leads to exclusion from society. But note that the death penalty is withheld.

Cain is punished but protected. Hope remains. Even Cain can be saved.

For further reading

Hebrews 11:4; 12:24; Luke 10:29–37

The myth of the Flood   Genesis 6:5—9:17

These stories have many levels of truth, all clearly seen in the story of the Flood.

One level is historical. When Sir Leonard Woolley excavated the city of Ur in Mesopotamia, he dug through many layers of civilization built one on top of the other. Then he came to a layer of mud without any human artifacts. He thought he had reached the bottom, but something drove him on to dig further. Lower still, he uncovered another civilization totally different from those above. He concluded that a period of extraordinary rainfall had caused the Tigris and Euphrates to overflow and flood the plain which, at the time, was the whole of the known world.

This would explain why the story of the Flood is found in the writings of other civilizations, including the story of a family saved from drowning by building a boat. There is, therefore, a factual basis to the story, roughly dated 4000BC.

Then there is the level of literary criticism. It is quite likely that the Jews, exiled in Babylon, would know about the Babylonian story. Their own story, with infinitely greater depth of meaning, had two versions. These differed in minor details, such as the number of days it rained. Not knowing which version to use, the Jewish compilers threaded the two versions together. This explains the minor inconsistencies and repetition.

The important level is the religious one. As we listen to the daily news, with its diet of awfulness, don't we sometimes think, 'Oh God, what a mess. Why not admit your creation is a failure, and wash it out?' But over and over again the Bible shows God creating good out of evil, if he can find just one person willing to trust and obey him. What a crazy idea, to build a huge boat in the middle of a dry plain. But Noah was willing to be God's fool. He built the boat, and so became the means of saving, not just his family, but humanity as well as all living creatures.

Noah is not a Jew, but in chapter 5—oh these boring begats!—he is linked with Adam, the father of all mankind. In chapter 11—still more of them—he is linked to Abraham who, according to St Paul, is the father of all the faithful, both Jew and Gentile. Noah's story is our story. Since we are threatened by the flood of evil engulfing our world, God calls us by faith not just to save ourselves, but become the means of bringing his salvation to others too. The story foreshadows God's plan of salvation. What profoundly meaningful images it uses:

▷ *The ark, God's lifeboat, now a logo for the ecumenical Church (Hebrews 11:7)*

▷ *The Flood, force of destruction, chaos returning, but used by God to baptize his people and cleanse them from sin*

▷ *The animals, forced to live in harmony again, as they did in Eden, and as they will again in the kingdom of the Messiah (Isaiah 11:9)*

▷ *The dove, symbol of God's Spirit, pledge of hope, bearing the olive branch of peace (Ephesians 1:13–14)*

▷ *The rainbow, sign of God's everlasting mercy, seen in John's vision shining above God's throne (Revelation 4:3)*

This is the first of four covenants God makes in the Bible. It is the only one made with all mankind, and it has no conditions attached (Isaiah 54:9–10).

Then comes the folk story of Noah's drunkenness (Genesis 9:21–27). You may wonder at the inclusion of this nasty story. It does however, show that experience of salvation does not guarantee we won't commit sins in the future—a useful warning. The sordid details about Ham, the ancestor of the Canaanites, reflect the hatred the Jews had for the obscene practices of Canaanite worship.

For further reading

Matthew 24:36–39; Hebrews 11:6–7; 1 Peter 3:18–22

The myth of the tower of Babel   Genesis 11:1–9

The idea of the tower of Babel may have come from the ziggurats, the stepped pyramids of Assyria and Babylon. Like the pyramids of Egypt they represented the pride of ancient empires whose kings sought immortality. Today, the skyscrapers of a modern city symbolize the pride of men's economic empires. Adam's sin has spread to infect the nations, which seek the power and glory belonging properly to God. 'Go to,' say these ambitious men. 'Let us build and make a name for ourselves.'

'Go to,' echoes God, as he goes down to confound them. Superficially this is an explanation for the diversity of language. But we do not need to speak different languages to misunderstand each other. A mathematician, a poet, a farmer and a priest will all speak a different language. At a deeper level our self-concern acts as a barrier to communication. We wear masks to hide from each other. We distort what others say. Words become camouflage. We are adept at propaganda and disinformation.

Throughout history and in our own time, people have tried to set up communities. Those not founded on devotion to God break up because the members can't get on. Individuals try to dominate and get overthrown by others. It is by the mercy of God that he allows such divisive forces to drive us apart, otherwise we would enslave each other. Even a church can become tyrannous. Perhaps this is why God allows our 'unhappy divisions' to continue!

Felix culpa—happy sin

A case can be made against God for being himself the cause of Adam's fall. Why put a tree in the garden if it was to be out of bounds? To say, 'Don't eat' has the same effect as a notice, 'Keep off the grass'. It is positively an invitation to disobey.

Here is a paradox, beautifully expressed in the fifteenth-century carol 'Adam lay y-bounden', and in the phrase *felix culpa*—happy sin.

The innocence of ignorance is of little value, if any. Cows are content. We have 'immortal longings', and discontent drives us to rebel. Adolescent rebellion is a necessary stage on the way to maturity. It is as we struggle with sin that we come to know God, and experience the joy of salvation—a joy the angels envy! (1 Peter 1:12). The prodigal son ended up closer to his father than his law-abiding brother. See also Luke 7:44–47.

God foresaw all this. His plan for our salvation through Jesus Christ was adopted even before our creation! (Ephesians 1:3–6).

For further reading

Luke 1:46–51; 1 Corinthians 1:26–29

For group discussion

1. Can any good come out of natural disaster?

2. Am I my brother's keeper?

3. To see the Church as an ark of salvation can lead to distortion. What other images are needed to redress the balance?

For private reflection

1. How do you relate science to faith?

2. What difference does the naming of animals make to our relationship with them?

3. What alienates people from God today?

2

The Call and the Promise

Genesis 12–50

We now move on to Act One of the Bible drama. Its theme is God's plan of salvation through the call of a chosen people. In the rest of the book of Genesis we see how such a people came into being.

Abraham   *Genesis 11:27–25:10*

It began with the call of Abraham, the father not just of the Jewish race, but of all God's faithful people (Galatians 3:6–7). His call and pilgrimage throws light upon our own. We travel in his footsteps.

Abraham's call   Genesis 12:1–9

Abraham grew up in Ur, a trading seaport, and centre of a great civilization. He was wealthy, and quite old when the call came, and he had already been uprooted by his father Terah (Genesis 15:7). It looks as if Terah had been called to leave Ur and enter Canaan. He started the journey but settled down in Haran. Did he find the going too tough for an old man?

Abraham was well settled down when his call came. 'Get out, leave home. Go to an unknown land that I will show you. Then you will not only be blessed yourself but will be a blessing to all the families on earth.'

It must have sounded crazy. What a challenge! What a risk! Such a command and promise from an unknown, unseen God, known only by his word.

How did Abraham hear it? How do we? Very occasionally it is audible. Mostly it consists of words forming in our mind with continuous insistence. It doesn't seem to be coming from ourselves, but we can't be sure. To obey is always an act of faith. But it is by such faith, such obedience, we come into a right relationship with God, not by being religious and doing a lot of good deeds (Hebrews 11:8).

Abraham obeyed the command and believed the promise. He and his family entered Canaan, and travelled through it. It was enemy-occupied territory. Wherever he camped he built an altar and prayed. He was

24

consecrating it as a holy land. In the same way we can consecrate our homes and the places where we work and visit.

Abraham in Egypt

To say 'Yes' to God's call, and to start out on our pilgrimage doesn't mean we won't ever commit sins or make mistakes! This story, retold in another version in chapters 20 and 26, makes this quite clear. In those days, things being as they were, Abraham had good reason for fear, but why was he in that situation? God did not send him. If Abraham had trusted God to meet his needs he wouldn't have been in a place where he was tempted to lie, and worse. Pharaoh was more moral than Abraham—unbelievers often are! As in the story of Jonah, the point is made that, when God's people sin, they get others into trouble. God uses unbelievers to rebuke us.

The surrender of choice
Genesis 13

The flocks of Abraham and Lot multiply. With enemies around them, conflict between their herdsmen over water was a potential danger. It was best to part. Abraham had the elder's right of choice. He surrenders it to his nephew.

Lot looks down on the lush pastures of the plain. Life would be easier there. And there were cities. True, they had a bad reputation. He didn't need to live in them, or share their evil ways. It would be nice just to be near, shop in their markets, and enjoy a bit of culture and civilization again. So he turns his back on the land of promise, leaves the hills, and descends to the plain.

Abraham stayed put, waiting for God to guide him (Hebrews 11:13–16). He is told to look in all directions. The promise is repeated—for the third time—this is the land for him and his descendants. Told to move on, Abraham goes to Hebron, where again he builds an altar, consecrating the place to God.

Abraham's meeting with Melchizedek
Genesis 14

The result of Lot's choice of ease and prosperity was the opposite—war and capture. Abraham had to go and fight to rescue him. After the battle he met a mysterious character, Melchizedek, high priest and king of righteousness. Salem, identified with Jerusalem, means peace—*salaam*, *shalom*.

As priest of the Most High God who gave Abraham victory, he blesses Abraham and offers him bread and wine.

What a strange foreshadowing of Jesus Christ! The writer of the book of Hebrews makes much of this (Hebrews 6:19–7:28). Was Christ, the eternal Word, really there?! (See John 8:56–58.)

The promise depended upon Abraham being able to father a son. He and his wife were old and childless. Was the problem to be solved by adoption? 'No', says God. And Abraham believes, but asks for the reassurance of a sign.

God in reply makes a solemn covenant with him. In ancient times a covenant was made by the two parties to it walking between the two halves of a slaughtered animal, and calling down on themselves the fate of the victim should they violate the agreement. This explains 15:9–10.

Abraham, in a deep sleep, senses God's presence. There is darkness filling him with awe and terror, as he learns of the long years of slavery his people will suffer. Then a cloud of fire, symbol of God's presence, passes between the carcases, and the covenant with Abraham is made.

Note the golden verse 15:1 and compare it with Psalm 73:25–26.

So often, after a high peak of spiritual experience, one comes down to earth with a bump. This is the time when temptation attacks.

Sarah doesn't believe what is humanly impossible. She is long past child-bearing, so she tells Abraham to have a son by her servant Hagar. Abraham, instead of listening to God, listens to Sarah. It sounded so sensible. It was in fact disastrous. When the plan succeeds, the old monster of jealousy takes possession of Sarah, and only the angel of the Lord—God himself in visible form—saved Hagar and her son, not once but twice (Genesis 16:4–16; 21:9–21).

Abraham had to wait thirteen long painful years of unfulfillment before God spoke again. Then God's first words were, 'Live in my presence, be perfect' (NJB). Which meant, 'Let your faith and obedience be without interruption.' Forgiveness is shown by both Abraham and Sarah being given new names. Previously they had been Abram and Sarai; Sarah means princess. Also the covenant is renewed with the visible and permanent mark of circumcision. A clear cut was to be made by those who were God's people. They were to be separate, set aside for God's use, which is what the words 'holy' and 'sacred' mean. This is what is implied by the sign of the cross often made on the forehead at baptism. Hindus show their commitment to their gods by marking their foreheads with ash. Today, some Christians like to wear a cross, or a fish, to proclaim their allegiance. But circumcision was not optional!

Genesis 15:6 was used by St Paul to show that God accepts us on the basis of faith, not on the action of circumcision, which some Jewish Christians were trying to force on Gentile converts (Romans 4:18–24; Galatians 3:6).

Entertaining angels unaware   Genesis 18

The next incident is very mysterious. First we are told that the Lord
appeared to Abraham and then that three strangers appear. The famous
icon by Rublev of three sitting round a table, identical in face, is
sometimes called 'The Hospitality of Abraham' and sometimes 'The
Holy Trinity'. It is both. It is a hot mid-afternoon—rest hour—when the
visitors arrive as total strangers. With what haste and generosity Abraham
offers hospitality. A 'morsel of bread' forsooth!

After the meal they call for Sarah and promise her a son. A direct vision of
the Lord might have terrified her. As it was she laughed. Less well known is
that Abraham too had laughed with disbelief (17:17). For himself he could
believe but not for her!

'Is anything too hard for the Lord?' What answer would—do—we give
to such a question? Sarah daren't say 'Yes' or 'No'. So she evades, and
denies that she laughed. But the Lord insists, 'You did laugh.'

The text swings from 'the men' to 'the Lord'. In this scene from John
Houston's film, *The Bible*, Peter O'Toole played all three men. They are
going to visit Sodom before overthrowing it. They go, but Abraham is still
with the Lord. The Lord shows his trust in Abraham by confiding his
purpose to him. He is to become father of a people called to be God's
channels of salvation. Will they care for the world, or only for themselves?
Abraham cares. He pleads with God for Sodom. God is more than willing
to be pleaded with. The city will be saved if only ten faithful people can be
found in it. It was the survival of a tiny remnant of faith that made Christ's
coming possible (Luke 2:25, 36–37). A family can be saved through one
faithful member. A parish can be revived by a handful of praying people.
Nations were transformed by men like Luther and Wesley.

The fall of Sodom   Genesis 19

Lot is again involved. From living on the outskirts, he had been sucked
into the city, though he tried to keep himself separate from it. In spite of
the night's horrible experience, and the warning of his visitors, he doesn't
want to leave. Finally he goes, but his wife looks back and is turned into a
pillar of salt, a detail added perhaps to explain such a pillar, still common
to the area.

Pompeii offers a more literal alternative suggestion! What matters
however is its warning, repeated by Jesus, about the danger of looking
back (Luke 9:62).

Even now Lot begs to be allowed to retire to Zoar, another city, 'only a
little one'. Permission is given, but he is soon frightened into leaving it
and returning to the mountains. Sin can offer great attraction, but it can
develop into something so dangerous that we are frightened back to
God, who is too gracious to refuse to welcome us back.

The impossible happened. Sarah conceived and bore her son. The name Isaac means 'God laughed'. He certainly had the laugh on Sarah. Do we believe God has a sense of humour?

When Isaac was grown—the Jewish age of responsibility being twelve—Abraham's faith was put to its final and hardest test.

Human sacrifice was a common practice and continued to be so amongst the surrounding nations for thousands of years. We must not read into Abraham's mind the horror we feel. God is not cruel, it is men who think him so, making him an image of themselves. This experience taught Abraham and his descendants that God does not want human sacrifice. Later, prophets would teach that he does not want animal sacrifice either, though not all Jews accepted this.

Abraham's anguish was partly due to his love for his dear son, his only son. Even more it was due to the agony of wondering why God, who had at last so wonderfully given Isaac, should now take him away. How could the promise be fulfilled?

It was only because Abraham had, for so many years, made a habit of believing and obeying God, that he was able to trust now without any sign of hesitation. He had learnt what it meant to be a friend of God (2 Chronicles 20:7). So he was ready to make the supreme sacrifice of giving to God what he valued most, more than his own life. He gave his son back to God, believing that both Isaac and the promise could be safely left in his hands. On such staggering faith our salvation depended and our own faith has been built (Hebrews 11:17–19).

Nearly two thousand years later God gave his only and beloved Son as a sacrifice. Like Isaac, Jesus carried the wood for his self-offering up the mountain. Mount Moriah is believed to be the site of the Jewish temple where the Dome of the Rock now stands. The Lamb which God provided died on Calvary, less than a furlong away! For Jesus there was no last-minute rescue.

Abraham received his son back, together with the sixth renewal of the promise. Isaac must have been still more precious. Parents who give their children to God receive them back with joy more often than those who clutch hold of them as their own possession. As with our own life, to cling is to lose. To give is to receive (Luke 9:24).

Finding Isaac a wife   Genesis 24

Sarah died and was buried at Hebron. The land does not yet belong to Abraham and he buys a cave there from its owner. Note his extreme courtesy (23:1–7, 10–13). In the Middle East, one's homeland is the place where one's ancestors are buried.

Abraham's last task is to find a wife for Isaac. The story of how he sent his servant to look for a bride amongst his kinsmen in Haran is a beautiful one, illustrating the 'coincidences' that so often happen when we allow the Spirit to guide us.

To the writer, as to Abraham, what is of supreme importance is that the bride should be of the household of faith. All through their long history, the people of God were led into idolatry, and its resulting evils, through intermarriage with pagan women. St Paul warned of a similar danger to Christians. If husband and wife are to be 'one flesh' they also need to be of one heart and one spirit (2 Corinthians 6:14). Difference in other matters can create richness and variety, but differences in the basic direction of one's life leads to strife, stalemate—a significant word—and probably nowadays to divorce (Amos 3:3).

Abraham died and was buried with his wife at Hebron. Both Isaac and Ishmael were together at the ceremony. Herod the Great built a huge building over what is believed to be the spot. It is now a mosque, but a couple of rooms are set aside for Jews. Today Jews and Arabs meet there daily for worship, but the hostility between the descendants of Abraham's two sons continues. Hebron is a flashpoint that today threatens the peace of the world.

Jacob: the choice of a cheat   *Genesis 27–35*

Little more is known about Isaac except that he dug wells—almost as important in fact and symbol as altars. He had to fight to hold onto them, but finally succeeded and made peace with his neighbours.

Jacob, however, is a character drawn in depth. It is a problem to many that God should choose a crafty customer like Jacob in place of an easy-going outdoor sort of fellow like Esau who is more likeable and wins our sympathy.

> *How odd of God to choose the Jews.*
> *Oh no it's not. He knows what's what.*

This couplet has it in a nutshell.

The man to be trusted with the promise and blessing must be one who appreciates its importance, and has the tenacity to hold on at any cost.

Over and over again we find that God is able to do business with the rebel and the sinner, however bad, but not with the indifferent, however nice (Revelation 3:16). Rebels can be reformed and sinners saved. Nice people see no need for either process.

Notice how God deals with Jacob step by step.

The first encounter is when Jacob has touched bottom, fleeing from home, lonely and sleeping rough. He dreams of a ladder linking earth and heaven. Jesus was to compare himself to this ladder (John 1:51). God, at the top of it, gives Jacob the promise he gave to Abraham, together with a personal promise of protection and guidance.

'The Lord is in this place; and I did not know it.' Such an experience of God is like the light coming on behind the gauze curtain in pantomime or ballet. Behind it we see wonderful beings of another world. When the light goes out they disappear, but we know they were there before we saw them, and are there still.

Jacob vows that, if God indeed brings him home safely, he will accept God as his God, and give him a tithe. Despite his vision, he is still a bargainer. God's work on him has only begun. But how many of his critics pay God a tenth of their income?

Jacob reaches Haran, and, for him too, 'coincidences' begin. At a well he meets Rebekah and falls in love with her. She is the daughter of his uncle for whom he was looking! She takes him home with her.

Laban is a bargainer too, equally given to deceit.

For the next fourteen years, Jacob is paid back in his own coin. But God blesses him with prosperity, and Jacob learns patience.

As a skilful breeder of sheep, Jacob counters Laban's trickery with tricks of his own. The methods he uses are unimportant! When he decides on flight he takes no more than what he reasons is his due. Laban pursues, and is only stopped from violence by a dream. The two men are so alike. Diamond cuts diamond. After a long noisy set-to, full of self-justification and mutual reproach, they finally make a covenant and part in peace.

Jacob learns that Esau is coming to meet him. He presumes he is set on delayed revenge, and is afraid. His first reaction is practical. He divides his people and flocks into two, hoping that, if one is attacked, the other will be safe. Only his second reaction is to pray, but there is a new humility in his prayer, which has no trace of bargaining.

He then attempts appeasement by sending ahead herds and flocks of sheep to buy off Esau's anger. Lastly, he takes steps to see his wives and children are safe.

Now he is left alone, and he spends the whole night wrestling with God.

This is one of the deepest and most mysterious passages of the Old Testament. Only those who have themselves wrestled with God can begin to understand it.

Jacob clings on all night. He will not let go until he is blessed. Surprisingly, it is Jacob who prevails, though the cost of such battling marks him for life. God honours his victory by the award of a new name. No longer Jacob the deceiver, from now on he is to be Israel, God's warrior. God does not need to tell Jacob his name. Jacob knows who it is. The name is only later disclosed to Moses.

When Jacob meets his brother, he is a new man. He greets his brother with humility and, to his surprise, Esau welcomes him with friendliness.

Jacob is safely home. God, as always, has kept his promise.

Joseph: how evil is turned into good   *Genesis 37–50*

If the story of Jacob shows how God deals with a baddie, in that of Joseph we see him dealing with a goody, if not a goody-goody.

It wasn't Joseph's fault. The beloved son of the beloved wife, he was petted and spoilt by his father, who openly preferred and favoured him. He even trained him to act as a tell-tale. No wonder Joseph's brothers were jealous and hated him. Yet, in how many families today, parents show such particular favour, if only verbally with special praise or blame, not realizing the harm they do, and the consequences of damaging relationships.

The story shows clearly the weaving together of two versions of the story. In one Reuben is more important. He plans to save Joseph from the pit, but isn't there to prevent him being sold to the Midianites. It is Reuben who sees Joseph's harsh treatment of them in Egypt as a punishment for their lack of mercy to him, thus reducing Joseph to tears. And it is Reuben who pledges his children against Benjamin's safe return. In the other version Judah saves Joseph from death and arranges for his sale to Ishmaelites. Judah pledges himself for Benjamin's safety, and, by offering to take Benjamin's place as Joseph's slave, opens the floodgates of Joseph's tears and his self-disclosure.

But the central character is Joseph. Three times he suffers the heavy blows of fortune. First his brothers plan to kill him, but instead sell him as a slave into Egypt. There he rises to become a trusted steward in his master's house, but his moral integrity turns the lust of his master's wife into hatred, and her lies land him in jail. Lastly, after his interpretation of the butler's dream proves true, the butler forgets his promise to speak to Pharaoh to get his release. No mere goody-goody could have survived. Joseph's faith is rock-like. He retains his integrity and his faith. His experiences lead him to discover he is not just a dreamer, but a born administrator, with the natural authority that wins respect.

The problem of Pharaoh's dream brings Joseph back to the butler's mind. Joseph not only interprets Pharaoh's dream, giving all the glory for this to God, but ventures to offer such wise advice that he is put in charge of storage and famine relief, and given top-ranking authority in the kingdom! He marries and has children. He thanks God that now at last he is able to forget the past. But has he?

What irony! What we don't forgive we don't forget. Unexpectedly confronted by his brothers, all Joseph's repressed rage erupts. He shouts at them, and, to their total incomprehension, claps them in prison. After three days he calms down and is able to think. He knows revenge is wrong. What he really wants is to see his own brother Benjamin again. He decides to let them all go, keeping only Simeon in prison as pledge of Benjamin's coming and their return. Why Simeon? On the basis of Simeon's reputation for cruelty (Genesis 49:5 also 34:25) it is likely that he was the one to plot Joseph's death. With what psychological under-standing the story unfolds the costly and often long process of full forgiveness.

When the brothers return with Benjamin, after battling with their father, Joseph is ready to treat them well, and feasts them, astonishing them with his apparently supernatural knowledge of their respective ages. Then he works out a plot by which they can all be sent home leaving Benjamin behind. He may have said to himself, as many do today, 'I have forgiven them but I never want to see them again.' The plot fails. Joseph hadn't expected his brothers to care so much, either for Benjamin or their father. Judah's self-offering breaks down the final barrier. It is not only Joseph who has changed. They have too. How easy it is to judge people by what they have been! How lovingly he now embraces them, and plans for their settlement in Egypt.

But reconciliation is two-way. Joseph has now forgiven from his heart, but the brothers are not sure of this. They are afraid. 'Maybe Joseph will take his revenge.' When Israel dies they dare not even see Joseph without sending him a message begging again for forgiveness. In Joseph's response the theme of the story is revealed. 'Ye thought evil against me; but God meant it unto good ... to save much people alive' (Genesis 50:20 AV). He had said this before, but, in the tumult of emotion, they had not taken it in (Genesis 45:5–8). Here is a golden thread of truth that shines in its fullest glory from the cross. Though we must take responsibility for the evil we do, God is in it, suffering, healing and using it as a blessing for us. Mysteriously, evil is part of God's plan. Herein lies our hope (Romans 5:3–5; 8:28).

So the book of Genesis ends. The twelve tribes of Israel, God's holy people, have come into being in fulfilment of God's promise.

The land of promise has been explored, hallowed by altars and claimed by the digging of wells and the burying of ancestors. But people and land are left separated, far apart.

The blessing of Joseph's two sons (chapter 48) explains why they take the place of Joseph in the parcelling out of the land of Canaan. Levi, as the priestly tribe, was landless.

Scene One of this great drama points forward to Scene Two—the exodus.

For further reading

Hebrews 11:8–22; John 8:33–59; Galatians 3:1–16; 4:21–31

For group discussion

1. Faith means taking risks. What risks have you taken or has the Church taken?

2. What difference would it make to see your children as belonging primarily to God?

3. Conversion can be a sudden or long drawn-out experience. Compare your experiences in the group.

For private reflection

1. A calling, a pilgrimage, an adventure of faith: how do you see your life?

2. Jacob had the right priorities. What are yours?

3. Why is it so hard to forgive? What makes it possible?

3

Moses and the Exodus from Egypt

Exodus; Numbers

We now come to the great event that, for the Jews, has been the basis of their faith and the explanation of their history.

By a series of mighty acts God delivered the Hebrew slaves out of Egypt and brought them into Canaan, their Promised Land, as a free people.

God chose for his purpose a people downtrodden, exploited, despised and helpless, utterly dependent upon him. They were called to witness to all peoples the glory of God and his power to save (Deuteronomy 7:6–7; 8:11–18; compare 1 Corinthians 1:27–29; 1 Peter 2:9–10).

Today, oppressed Black and South American Christians identify with this story and see God as siding with them in their struggles for freedom. This is what Black theology and liberation theology are about.

Moses: the man of two worlds   *Exodus 1–2*

The descendants of Israel multiplied. Fear led the Egyptians to enslave them, and make the first recorded attempt at genocide.

Like Herod, over a thousand years later, they learnt that God does not allow his purposes to be frustrated. Again, God had the last laugh. Moses, like Noah, is saved by an act of faith in a miniature ark, and, with what irony, he is adopted by Pharaoh's daughter and brought up at court! The pharaoh concerned was probably Rameses II (early thirteenth century BC). On the walls of the cities he built are wall paintings showing Semitic slaves making bricks.

When and how did Moses learn who he was? This is a fascinating source of speculation. His sudden act of violence (Exodus 2:11–12) suggests he may have only just have learnt about it. Such cruelty was a daily event, but had not previously led to such reaction. That day, Moses is shocked into identifying not with the Egyptian overseer but the Hebrew slave, and he commits murder. Later, while trying to pacify two quarrelling slaves he finds that his murder had been witnessed. The slaves, instead of welcoming his effort to defend them, distrust and reject him. Had they always known he was a Hebrew?

Moses fled. He may have had other options. He could have begged pardon from Pharaoh on the grounds that his violent act was due to the sudden shock of learning of his origin. He could have remained a loyal Egyptian, using what influence he had at court to alleviate the slaves' condition. The writer of the Book of Hebrews had other ideas powerfully relevant today (Hebrews 11:24–27). Many seek to improve the condition of the poor. Few, like Mother Teresa, identify themselves with their poverty and suffering.

The call of Moses   *Exodus 3–4*

From the privileged life of an autocratic prince, Moses learns how to be a shepherd. Long years of looking after sheep taught him the patience he was to need as leader of the cantankerous children of Israel.

The burning bush is essentially an experience of God. Fire is a powerful symbol of God, his glory and beauty, his purifying holiness, his energizing power. Potentially dangerous, it is under control. The bush is not consumed. Moses stops in his tracks, turns and looks. So, when God calls, he can respond, 'Here am I.' God does not compel our attention or our recognition, but his call is always personal—'Moses, Moses!' A Middle Eastern shepherd knew his sheep by name (John 10:3). God is the good shepherd who calls us by name.

Moses must have brooded over the plight of his people, and his failure to help them. Now he learns that God not only knows and cares about their plight, but plans to do something to rescue them. The shock comes when Moses learns he is being called by God to act on his behalf.

Moses makes excuses, four of them, typical of our own. Evasion dresses up as humility—'Who am I?' Ignorance of God, fear of rejection and failure, lack of talent for public speaking, God patiently deals with all these. But when Moses ends up by saying, 'Find someone else,' God is angry. The only valid excuse is the plea that Moses doesn't know God's name. In Hebrew the name implies the character. 'I am that I am' also means 'I am what I will be'. The knowledge of God is progressive. He is beyond all definition. We learn to know him as we live with him in daily faith and obedience.

The Hebrew word *YHWH*, probably pronounced *Yahweh*, was considered too holy to say, so the Jews instead used the word *Adonai* meaning the Lord.

Moses, with Jethro's blessing, sets out on his mission. God's 'coincidences' begin. Aaron has already left Egypt and set out to look for Moses! Pharaoh (Rameses?) is dead. The new pharaoh (Mernepha?) would, in Moses' childhood memories, be his half-brother. Moses shares his experience and he and Aaron set off back into Egypt together.

What are we to make of verses 24–26? A primitive fragment of ancient legend? Why should the compiler retain it? Was it to emphasize the importance of circumcision and the desire to link it to Moses? Maybe. So often, as with the story of Jacob's night of wrestling, it is the strangest texts that provide the deepest insights.

Circumcision was, as we have seen, a sacrament of total commitment to God, a dying to self, without which Moses could not have succeeded in his mission.

In Zipporah's reproach we can see, not just a mother's pity for her son, but the jealous hostility of a husband or wife when the partner, after an experience of God's call, makes a costly commitment similar to that of Moses.

The exodus: plagues and Passover   *Exodus 5–15*

At first there was success. The slaves gave Moses and Aaron a good reception. They believed and worshipped God. Pharaoh however, who would remember Moses as a traitor, reacted with defiant contempt. By doubling the slaves' labour he turned them against their would-be liberators. 'Why?' cries Moses, anguished and perplexed.

'God hardened Pharaoh's heart' is a text that creates a problem for us. It is part of the problem and the ambivalence of evil. The sun creates shadows. Freedom for good creates freedom for rejection of good (Isaiah 45:7).

How free are we? Like Pharaoh, most of us react to circumstances according to our upbringing and self-interest. Without the inspiration of God's Spirit we are predictable. Pharaoh's servants read the signs before he did. We are free to open or shut our minds to new truth if it is convenient. Pharaoh chose to resist. Looking back, the Chronicler saw how this led to the signs that glorified God, and bound the Israelites to him with a strong cord of faith. Victory is neither glorious nor decisive if it is a walkover. The problem verse is the Chronicler's way of expressing this. As we have seen in the story of Joseph, God uses evil to advance his purposes. What hope that gives us today!

The plagues are all natural events. As Neil's commentary points out, the discolouration of the Nile by red marl carried down from Abyssinia, the swarm of frogs, flies and locusts, cattle disease and sand storms darkening the sky, are all common to Egypt, though not to Palestine, home of the narrator, where only the hail would be experienced and the other plagues unknown. Volcanic action has even been suggested. It could poison the Nile and set up a chain of such disasters, leading to a series of epidemics. The slave camp at Goshen was sufficiently distant and isolated to escape.

All this does not mean that God was not at work. The combination of natural events, their ferocity, and their timing must have seemed miraculous. Only something overwhelming would have compelled Pharaoh to allow the slaves to depart. Israel believed it was God's deliverance, and this belief shaped their religion, and the rest of their history.

It may be that three versions of the story have been strung together here. One of them stresses the magic used both by Moses and Pharaoh's magicians. But magic is an unconvincing argument. Another version stresses Aaron's role. The five chapters (7–11) can seem tediously repetitious, but, while skipping through them, note two things.

First, again as Neil's commentary points out, this is not just God's battle with Egypt's king but with Egypt's gods. The holy Nile, with its sacred crocodiles, is contaminated. The cattle, objects of worship as in India today, are destroyed by disease, and the magicians, servants of the gods, break out in boils. Finally, the sun god, Amon Ra, Egypt's principal deity, is blotted out by 'a darkness that could be felt'. What a pregnant phrase!

Secondly, there is a dramatic progression. The contest has five rounds. In the first (7:8—8:32), the magicians admit defeat, and division is made between the land where the Egyptians live and the slave ghetto. Pharaoh only agrees to allow them to worship God in Egypt.

In round two (9:1–35), his servants are divided, as some believe in the signs and are saved from damage. Pharaoh is forced to admit to sin. In round three his servants force him to allow at least the men to go. After the darkness, round four (10:21–29), Pharaoh has to agree to all going, but without their animals. After this, confrontation is broken off on both sides.

The last straw was the plague that brought death to the children. The horror of this tragedy brought liberation. So often in history the powers that be only surrender after such a price has been paid. Like children today, it is the most innocent and most vulnerable that pay the price of people's sins.

The Passover and its memorial   Exodus 12–13; 16

The lamb is killed. Its blood is smeared on the door posts. Its flesh is eaten by the Hebrews packed and ready to go. There is no time for the dough to rise.

In all this Christ's sacrifice is foreshadowed. His death saves us from the bondage and death of sin. His body and blood strengthen us for our own pilgrimage to the Promised Land. Jesus very carefully timed his death to coincide with the Passover. St John even notes the significant detail that not a bone of his body was broken (John 19:36; compare Exodus 12:46).

The event is to be celebrated every year—Jews and Christians do so to this day on Passover and on Good Friday. As Paul put it, 'For even Christ our passover is sacrificed for us' (1 Corinthians 5:7).

The sea crossing   Exodus 13:17—15:22

Pharaoh, again changing his mind, gave chase. God protects his people, hiding and guiding them with a pillar of cloud by day and fire by night. These two powerful symbols of God's presence permeate the whole Bible, and strike deep chords of meaning for us today.

Some Christians are troubled by the idea of God destroying Pharaoh's army. Are they equally disturbed by the overthrow of Hitler's or that of Saddam Hussein? The crossing of the Red Sea was probably at one of the inland fresh water lakes north of Suez. Red Sea is a mistranslation. A wind of extraordinary violence might be able to drive back the waters to form a ford, but the timing of the event was miraculous. The 'Song of Miriam' is one of the oldest fragments in the Bible, and is possibly contemporary with the event. The amazing act of deliverance is constantly celebrated in the Psalms (for example, Psalms 66; 77; 81). St Paul likened it to baptism (1 Corinthians 10:1–2). It was a dying to the old life of slavery, to be born again to a new life with the freedom of sons and daughters.

The march to Sinai: lessons in trust   *Exodus 16–40*

Baptism, sadly, does not in itself transform our character. The Hebrews still had a slave mentality. When the going got rough they grumbled, hankering for the security of life in Egypt, its misery shrouded in a rosy haze. They resorted to Adam's servile weapon of blame. Their target was not Moses but God. Faith is matured by obedience, not by miracles. Their faith was childish, depending on their desires being met—pronto! When God delays delivery, we doubt!

The story of Marah and Elim has been used by Christians as an allegory. Spiritual life can be a stagnant pond, no inflow, no outflow, unfit to drink. Or it can be a spring of fresh water welling up to make all around it fruitful. In 2 Kings 2:19–22 a similar miracle of healing takes place using salt (compare John 7:37–38).

God provides for his people in deserts. Here was manna, a tiny plant that springs up after dew, and an influx of migrating birds. Bread and meat! As always, God's timing was perfect. The gift was spoilt by disobedience. Sometimes God lets us have our own way and suffer from it (Psalm 106:14–15). Greed led to rotting food, and the choice of hunger or an upset stomach.

The next grumble was about water. How can we criticize? The need was obvious, but the idea that resorting to prayer was the answer never entered their heads. Unlike us, they had almost no experience of God's trustworthiness. They were having to learn, fast.

The reason for God's anger with Moses is clearer in Numbers 20:1–13. God told Moses only to speak to the rock and it would produce water. Then the glory would be God's. As any geologist will know, as possibly Moses did, striking a rock in a particular place can lead to a flow of water. But Moses had not yet mastered his imperious temper. His patience snapped. He shouted at the people with rage, 'Must we fetch you water out of this rock?' Then he whacked the rock with his rod, the symbol of God's authority. His punishment seemed hard at the time, but later is proved a blessing. When the people were finally ready to enter Canaan, Moses was too old to go with them.

The next test was a battle. Battles are won by high morale, the product of faith. Such faith had to be built up before the people could safely enter Canaan. In this confrontation with the Amalekites, the first of many, they learnt their dependence on prayer in this area of life also (Exodus 17:8–16). Prayer itself is a battle. It needs endurance, and the kind of group support offered by Aaron and Hur. *Yahueh-Nissi* means 'the Lord is my banner'. So long as their captain's standard is seen flying on the battlefield, soldiers will have the courage to fight bravely. Christ is not only seen as our standard-bearer, he is also our manna, (John 6:32–35) and meat (John 6:55) and our rock (1 Corinthians 10:4) out of whose stricken side flows the water of life (John 19:34).

The burden of leading these contentious people was exhausting Moses. His father-in-law was horrified to see that Moses was trying to do everything himself. He tells Moses to delegate (Exodus 18). In Numbers 11:16–29 it is God who tells him to choose men as leaders, and trust them with responsibility. God himself will equip them with his Spirit. Note that the Spirit is not confined by human procedures (compare Acts 10:44–48). Unlike Joshua, and rigid churchmen throughout history, Moses rejoices in God's generosity, without a trace of jealousy. He will not quench the Spirit! (1 Thessalonians 5:19).

The Law and the covenant — *Exodus 19–21; 24*

The covenant God made with Abraham is now to be made with his descendants who, as promised, have multiplied into a nation. Unseen, yet like a mother eagle bearing her children, God has protected and guided them to Sinai. Here he will meet with them and make known his purpose for them. They are to be a nation of priests, bringing the world to God, a vocation now given to us (1 Peter 2:9).

It is irrelevant whether or not Sinai was volcanic. Geologists have found no evidence of this. The cloud and fire, as always, symbolize the majestic holiness of God. The trumpet is his summons, calling his people into his presence.

Some people are upset by the fearsomeness expressed in 19:12 and 21–24. Slaves hate and despise their masters. Their only discipline is fear of the lash. Suddenly set free they see freedom as licence to do as they please, but licence only leads to another form of slavery. Recent experience of liberation in Eastern Europe has shown the need for learning how to be free. Democracy depends on a long training process. A new schoolmaster, faced by a rabble of children brought up to resist authority, needs to impose his personal authority from the word go. At this point fear can be a healthy preventive (20:20).

Christians, taught to believe in a God of love, sometimes presume on his love, and take him too lightly. 'The fear of the Lord is the beginning of knowledge' is a proverb that is still true for us (Proverbs 1:7), though the fear is more of a sense of awe. God is still like a burning fire, and C.S. Lewis' Aslan is not a tame lion!

The Ten Commandments, in their shorter version (Deuteronomy 5:1–21), are probably as Moses taught them. They form the Law which is the basis for the covenant. What made them unique was the way they bonded together religion and morality, the duty to God and neighbours. In the ancient world laws for both existed but were unconnected. The Greek gods hardly set a pattern for moral behaviour! In his summary of the Law, Jesus made this unity clear, quoting Deuteronomy 6:4–5 and Leviticus 19:18. John sums it up forcefully in his epistle (1 John 4:20–21).

In Exodus 24 the covenant is made in a setting that resembles the mount of transfiguration (Mark 9:1–8).

At the foot of the mountain are the people. Moses reads them the commandments, which they promise to obey. The lamb is slain, and the blood of the covenant is sprinkled on the altar (representing God) and on the people. Sacrifice was not seen as the taking of life but the releasing of it. The life was in the blood (Leviticus 17:14). It is the life of the sacrificial lamb that unites, and makes an at-one-ment between God and humanity.

This is what Jesus meant when he said, 'This is my blood of the new covenant, which is poured out for many for the forgiveness of sins' (Matthew 26:27). For years he must have meditated on these verses, applying them to himself. This is why he foresaw and accepted death at the hand of the priests.

Moses now goes up the mountain, taking with him Aaron, Aaron's two sons, and the seventy elders. Part way up, they are given a vision of God, a glory, but not beyond their capacity to bear. They share a meal of bread and wine, a Holy Communion, another foreshadowing. Lastly Moses is called up into the cloud. There, in the darkness, he waits faithfully, until God chooses to speak. The thick darkness that envelopes God, the 'cloud of unknowing', as a medieval mystic calls it, is the mystery of God which human thought cannot penetrate. It is also a merciful protection from a glory that would blind us.

The golden calf   *Exodus 32*

Bible numbers are symbolic. Four is the number of earth. Ten denotes completion. Moses stayed in the mountain until God's teaching was completed.

It was a long time. The people lost faith in his return, and in his God. They bullied Aaron into making a god for them, one they could see. Such gods were givers of goodies but made no moral demands. The people worshipped, feasted, danced and indulged in an orgy of drinking and sex. Perhaps some of this may be a picture of later Canaanite worship.

Moses' anger again explodes. He smashes the tablets inscribed with God's commandments, and, with the rousing cry, 'Who is on the Lord's side?' summons the faithful Levites to a massacre.

Note that God did not call for any of this. But the people's sin was more than disobedience. It was apostasy. The whole future of the nation was at stake. As the Rushdie affair has shown, Muslims, even today, will kill those who renounce their faith—sometimes even members of their own family. We make God in our own image, ascribing to him our human savagery. It takes a lifetime for God to recreate us in his.

But Moses is no harsh fanatic. The next day he reproaches the people, and then, brokenhearted, goes back up the mountain to plead for their forgiveness. Like St Paul (Romans 9:1–3) he is willing for his own name to be blotted out of the book of life if only his people can be saved. God does not accept such substitution. Only Christ can atone for sin.

Restoration   *Exodus 32:35—34:17, 28–35*

God's loving concern for his people is to restore them. What we see as punishment is a part of this (Hebrews 12:5–13).

The first 'punishment' was plague. Some sins have an obvious connection with diseases, but all sin leads to a sickness of spirit. The pain and misery are like a red light warning us to change, or death may result (Romans 6:23). A second consequence we have all experienced is the withdrawal of our sense of God's presence. God does not desert us. His angels still protect, but the angel of his presence is not there. God calls us to strip off all superficiality and be truly and deeply sorry for our sins.

Moses now sets up a tent of meeting. It is pitched far away, but within sight of the camp. There, as people worship at a distance, Moses talks with God face to face.

This seems to contradict another tradition (Exodus 33:20) but there is truth in both. In Christ, we can come into God's presence and experience intimate relationship with him. But God, in his glory and holiness, remains awesome and unknowable. Moses prays for three things. First that God will stay close and guide him. Otherwise he will give up. God promises this. He knows Moses by name, that is through and through (compare John 10:3; Psalm 139:1–5).

Then Moses asks to see God's glory. The wonderful answer (33:19–23; 34:5–7) needs meditation, not comment.

Finally, Moses asks for the people to be pardoned. God then restores the broken relationship. New tablets of the commandments are given, and a new covenant is made. God promises to give success in the conquest of Canaan, but note his stern warnings against further idolatry. God will brook no rival to first place in our hearts and obedience (Matthew 6:24).

When Moses left the tent his face shone. He was unaware, but his people were so blinded, he had to wear a veil (Exodus 40:3; 2 Corinthians 3:7–18). God's glory does shine out of the faces of those who love Him. They are unaware but we can recognize them.

More stories of rebellion   *Numbers 12–17*

In these chapters we read more stories of rebellion against Moses' authority.

In Numbers 12 Aaron and Miriam, his brother and sister, resent his marriage to an Ethiopian. The problem of marriage with pagans only arose after the Israelites had entered Canaan, so this story is based on an anachronism. God is again shown as angry and punishing. He is drawn too much in the image of man. Moses, in his prayer for his people's forgiveness, is growing into the image of Christ. Note the astonishing comment of 12:3!

In Numbers 16 a similar rebellion is led by Korah, in which the Levites challenge the superiority of the Aaronic priesthood. This is also clearly anachronistic, a problem of a much later age. The punishment is spectacular. The story of Aaron's rod—Numbers 17—is similar. Stories of distant events seem to have been turned by the Chronicler into cautionary tales. For further information in the way narratives were edited by the Chronicler see Chapter 12, page 128. But they still can speak to us about the danger of spiritual ambition. From Synod to parish level, even in a prayer group, there can be rivalry over leadership. Whenever challenged, Moses does not assert his own authority. He brings the matter to God to solve.

In Numbers 13–14 we read of the men being sent to spy out the land of Canaan. They return to report that it is indeed a fruitful land, but is well defended with walled cities, and a race of giants is living there. Caleb calls on the people to advance, trusting God's promise. All the others, except Joshua, voice their fears. The people are discouraged and refuse to go. As usual they moan and say they'll return to Egypt. Moses and the men of faith pray and exhort, but only God saves them from a stoning.

Again Moses prays for the people, confident, because he has seen and experienced the mercy and long-suffering patience of God (Numbers 14:18; compare Exodus 34:6–7). God however, will not allow this generation to enter Canaan. Caleb and Joshua alone are exempt from this ban. Such an adventure calls for people of courage and faith. Perversely, the people now insist on going ahead. The result is predictable. Thus, a journey that could have taken only weeks now takes forty years. Escape from the land of bondage can be both speedy and spectacular. The journey to the Promised Land is hard and testing and can take a lifetime, a lifetime of learning to live in obedience to God's overshadowing cloud (Numbers 9:20–23).

For further reading

Psalms 77; 78; 81; 114; Hebrews 3; John 6:27–58

For group discussion

1. Does the worship in your church help you to experience the majesty and glory of God? If not, what is needed?

2. How can an understanding of the sacrificial lamb of the Passover and covenant deepen our understanding of the Eucharist?

3. By what sort of discipline does God train his Church today?

For private reflection

1. How can we identify with people we try to help?

2. What excuses do we make to God?

3. How is prayer a battle?

4

Rituals and Regulations: the Law of Moses

Exodus; Leviticus; Deuteronomy

We have skipped a lot of chapters in Exodus and Numbers. Together with Leviticus and Deuteronomy they give details of laws, both religious and secular.

This is where readers get bogged down and give up. The laws seem so boring and irrelevant. But dig into them and you'll find gold. They are relevant and influence both our life and worship today. The Good News Bible is helpful here. Most of these laws belong to a later age than that of Moses. Details of the tabernacle and the sacrifices describe the temple, or at least the shrine that preceded it. Most of the secular laws apply only to a settled agricultural community. The writers of these books ascribed all these laws to Moses, as revealed to him by God on Sinai. This gave them a divine authority.

How are we to interpret this? Similar claims are made for the laws of the Qur'an. Fundamentalist Muslims try to enforce them today. Without freedom to re-interpret and adjust them to a modern society, this creates big problems. They would say it is society that must change, not the law, and they have a point to make here.

The claim of divine inspiration cannot be simply dismissed. But God, who inspired the Law, inspires, through his Spirit, its interpretation to speak to our situation today. This is not to be confused with our own adjustment of it to justify our present lifestyle (Matthew 19:7–8).

The Law as given to Moses was probably just the Ten Commandments. On their principles all other laws were based. In the same way, on the principles of these laws many of our own have been based.

In Exodus 40 we read that Moses did everything exactly as he was shown. We are not bound by the Mosaic Law, but Jesus said he came to fulfil, not to destroy it (Matthew 5:17–18). He underlined its principles by quoting Deuteronomy 6:4–5 and Leviticus 19:18. Note that he knew these laws backwards! He interpreted freely according to the Spirit of love

(Matthew 5:21–48; Mark 10:2–9; compare 2 Corinthians 3:6).

The author of Hebrews refers to the religious laws as a pattern of heavenly design (Hebrews 9:23), and as shadows and images of good things to come (Hebrews 10:11). This is a statement of faith, based on experience. Divine inspiration is not a dogma to be enforced, but an innate truth to be recognized by those with spiritual perception (John 9:39–41).

It is from this standpoint that we will now look at these books and start panning for gold.

Laws concerning religion: duty to God

The tabernacle   Exodus 25—26; 35:4—38:31; 39:32—40:33

The tabernacle or tent of meeting was divided into two by a curtain or veil (Exodus 26:31–34). Beyond the veil was the Holy of Holies. Here was placed the ark, a box containing the two tablets of stone (Hebrews 9:3–4). On top was laid the mercy seat covered by the wings of two kneeling cherubim. It is here that, shrouded in darkness, God chose to communicate with his people (Exodus 25:21–22).

Note that both the tabernacle and ark were portable (25:13–15). God is not stationary. He moves at the head of his pilgrim people. He moves so fast and so continuously that church people, locked in their buildings and institutions, are usually left behind.

God's glory rests upon his law, and our obedience to it. Over this rests his mercy, which angels adore, though sometimes we sinners take it for granted! No-one was allowed into the Holy of Holies except the high priest, and he only entered once a year on the Day of Atonement. But, when Jesus died on the cross, Matthew tells us that the veil of the temple was torn in two (Matthew 27:50–51). The way to God's presence lies open to all through Jesus (Hebrews 10:19–22). Outside the veil was the area called the tent of the congregation. In the temple of Jesus' day it was divided into the Court of the Priests, nearest the sanctuary, then the Court of Israel, then the Court of the Women. Nearest the veil were three important furnishings. First, a table for the 'shewbread' (Exodus 25:23–30 AV), bread offered to God and eaten only by the priests. Today the consecrated bread is only given to God's consecrated people, who are all, in this sense, priests.

Then there was the lampstand or candlestick, with seven lamps, which Jews call the *Menorah* (Exodus 25:31–37).

At the centre was the altar of incense, which sanctified and carried the people's prayers to heaven (Exodus 40:5; Revelation 8:3–4). All these are found in churches today.

Outside the tabernacle was the Outer Court. Here was the altar for the burnt offerings (Exodus 27:1–8). Between this and the tabernacle stood a brass laver for washing. Today, in the porch of Catholic churches, a stoup of holy water is placed with which worshippers sign themselves with the cross as they enter. Sometimes their offerings are collected here to be brought up to the sanctuary later by the sidesmen. Jesus washed his disciples' feet before offering up his life for their salvation (Hebrews 10:8–9, 21–22; Psalm 43:3–4).

So we can see this pattern set on the mount has affected the design of our church buildings with their porch, baptistry, nave, chancel and sanctuary. The difference lies in that all may now progress from the Outer Court to the Holy of Holies.

This has in turn shaped the order of our worship. For instance, the Anglican liturgy starts with our praying for the Holy Spirit to 'cleanse the thoughts of our hearts'. A reading of the Law then leads us to confession of sin, and a prayer of absolution. There follows a sacrifice of praise and obedience as we sing the Gloria and listen to the reading and expounding of God's word in Scripture. This part of the service then comes to a climax in the creed, and a prayer of intercession for the world. Now the incense hallows us and our prayers, lifting them heavenwards. The bread is offered, and the consecration prayer starts with 'The Lord is here'. Christ the light of the world, stands in his risen power amid the candlesticks representing his Church (Revelation 1:12–13, 20). The Sanctus joins us to the worship of the angels (Revelation 4:5–8; cherubim had human heads, animals' bodies and eagles' wings). Finally, in the Holy Communion, we enter into the presence of God, and he enters into us!

The priests

Moses was a true priest. He stood before God in prayer on behalf of his people, and spoke to them on behalf of God thus acting as a mediator.

Moses was a Levite (Exodus 2:1–2). The whole tribe of Levi was given priestly duties to perform, but the actual priesthood was limited to the descendants of Aaron, Moses' brother (Numbers 16:8–11).

Christ is now our only mediator, but, as our high priest, he shares his priestly work with all his people. As Israel was a nation of priests so are we, the members of Christ's Church, which is his body (1 Peter 2:9). So all that follows has meaning for us.

The priestly robes   Exodus 28 (repeated in Exodus 39:1–31)

Note first the colours with which they were woven, gold, both precious and without alloy, blue, colour of the heavens, purple for royalty, scarlet for the blood of sacrifice.

The ephod, a straight linen sleeveless jacket, was joined at the shoulders by two onyx stones engraved with the names of the twelve tribes. Verse 12 explains why. Over the ephod is tied a breastplate. On this too are twelve precious stones, also representing the tribes (verses 15–21). When the priest stands before God he bears his people, precious to God however exasperating—on his shoulders as a responsibility, and on his heart as a burden of love.

Within the breastplate are the Urim and Thummim, stones that were used for deciding Yea or Nay in judgments. Judgments too must be made with a merciful and compassionate heart (verses 29–30). The hem of the ephod is hung with embroidered pomegranates and golden bells. These are to warn God of his coming, so that God will hide his glory, 'that he die not' (verses 33–35). For those who constantly handle holy things there is the danger of familiarity leading to presumption. Such bells are a warning to ourselves.

Finally, there is the mitre, a cap bearing a gold plate with the words 'Holiness to the Lord' (verses 36–38). Its meaning is expressed in the words of the prayer and hymn:

> *God be in my head, and in my understanding*

The consecration ceremony Exodus 29:1–35 (also Leviticus 8)

First is the washing, verse 4, a sign of confession and baptizing, a cleansing from sins.

Then comes the clothing. In many countries, after an adult baptism by immersion, the newly baptized will put on new clean clothes. We are given a robe of righteousness (Isaiah 61:6, 10; compare Zechariah 3:1–5). Only now is the priest fit to offer sacrifice.

The first sacrifice, of a bullock, is for his own sin. By laying his hands on it the priest transfers to it his sin. Priests are sinners like everyone else. Only Christ is a sinless priest (Exodus 29:11–14; Hebrews 7:25–28).

The second sacrifice, of a ram, is a burnt offering, verses 15–18. The sweet savour goes up to God as an offering of praise and thanksgiving.

Next comes the sacrifice of consecration (verses 19–21). The blood, representing the life of the victim, is released and is sprinkled on the priest's ear, thumb and toe. In some churches, after the water of baptism, a cross is marked with oil, representing baptism of the Spirit, on parts of a child's body. In churches where words are preferred to ritual actions, the anointing of candidates during a confirmation service might be covered by the singing of a hymn such as:

> *Take my life, and let it be*
> *Consecrated, Lord, to Thee.*

Finally there is the wave and heave offering of bread and meat. Part is given to feed the priests. Here is the offertory, which, in part, is for the support of the ministry.

Duties of the priest   Exodus 29:36—30:38

1. The daily sin offering (Exodus 29:36–37). We need to confess our sins and receive God's forgiveness every day.
2. The morning and evening sacrifice (Exodus 29:38–43). These are the times of special meeting with God, both for church congregations and for individuals.
3. Besides the sacrifice, which is an offering to God of worship, there is morning and evening the trimming of lamps and the burning of incense. Here is a picture of inflow and outflow. The virgins who trimmed their lamps (Matthew 25:4) had a constant supply of oil, which as we have seen, is a symbol of the Spirit. Incense carries our prayers up to God. Daily we receive from God, partly through meditating on Scripture. Daily we give out through our prayers for the world.
4. There is also a daily washing before any approach to God (Exodus 30:20–21) and a constant anointing, a constant renewal of consecration (verses 25–30).
5. Lastly a special perfume is prepared to fill the tabernacle with a sweet scent. It is not to be used by the priest. It is for God alone (verses 34–38). Where God is truly worshipped an atmosphere of holiness is created. In some churches, especially old ones, this can be very apparent. It can also be sensed in rooms and homes that have been steeped in prayer. The glory and beauty of it belongs wholly to God, not the occupant.

It is good to note that in Exodus (31:1–6) gifts of skilled craftsmanship, art and design, are gifts of God's Spirit. This would surely include the makers of stained glass, embroiderers of vestments, musicians, flower arrangers, and all who offer their skill with love and devotion to enhance the beauty of the house of God and our worship in it.

Fasts and festivals

There was, and still are, one main fast and three important feast days in the Jewish year.

The Day of Atonement   Leviticus 16

This was the solemn day of fasting and sacrifice for sin. It happened only once a year.

Individuals who sinned against the Law unintentionally could receive forgiveness after confessing their sin and making a trespass offering (Leviticus 4:1–12). The blood was sprinkled both on the altar of incense and the altar of offering where the fat was burnt. It was forbidden to eat both blood and fat, hence the importance of kosher meat for Jews today (Leviticus 3:17). The remains were burnt outside the camp. Here was a ritual symbolizing a renewal of the covenant relationship, an offering of praise, and a rejection of the old life.

For deliberate sin there was no forgiveness (Numbers 15:30–31). Even the author of Hebrews has doubts about this (Hebrews 10:26–29) but the sin referred to is 'treading under foot the Son of God', namely apostasy.

On the Day of Atonement the high priest sacrificed first a bullock for his own sin, and then one of two goats for the sin of his people. While the people waited outside the tabernacle, he first burnt incense to form a thick cloud and then, for this one occasion, he went behind the veil and sprinkled some of the blood on the mercy seat. He hallowed the Holy Place, for there is iniquity even in our holy things. Then he came out and sprinkled the rest of the blood on the altar in the courtyard, hallowing that too. Finally, in the sight of all the people, he laid his hands on the head of the live goat, and over it confessed all the people's sins. It was then led off into the wilderness, bearing their sins away.

Christ is the sacrifice whose blood atones for our sin. He is also our scapegoat. Isaiah prophesied this (Isaiah 53:4–6). St Paul recognized it (2 Corinthians 5:21). Surely Christ still suffers today in all the scapegoats on whom we place the blame for our own sins. All through the centuries the Jews have borne this burden.

The feast of the Passover   Leviticus 23:5–8

This was also called the feast of Unleavened Bread. Deuteronomy 16:3 explains that this was the 'bread of affliction' eaten on the night of the Passover, when the blood of the lamb saved them from death, and brought them their deliverance from slavery. This was annually remembered as it is today, but today the youngest child at the feast asks why things are done, and the father of the family answers. Jesus carefully planned his last meal with his disciples to coincide with the Passover. The bread and wine are given as his body and blood, sacrificed the next day. The feast of the Passover is celebrated by Christians on Maundy Thursday. (The Leviticus passage is repeated in Numbers 28:16–25; Deuteronomy 16:1–8.)

Pentecost: feast of the first fruits   Leviticus 23:9–14

Pentecost is a Greek word meaning fiftieth, and this feast, called Pentecost because it was held fifty days after the Passover, was a thanksgiving for the first fruits of the harvest. Deuteronomy 26:1–11 shows that every Israelite, in offering his gift, had to proclaim the great acts of God in bringing him to the land of Canaan. God chose this day for sending to his Church his gift of the Holy Spirit, the first fruit and pledge of our salvation (Ephesians 1:14). (The Leviticus passage is repeated in Numbers 28:26–31; Deuteronomy 26:1–11.)

The feast of Tabernacles   Leviticus 23:33–44

Preceded by the feast of Trumpets, this feast lasted a week (the details are repeated in Numbers 29). It was the harvest festival after the final ingathering. For this week they were to live in shelters or tents, as a reminder of their life in the desert. Jews in Israel do this today. How important it is, when wealth and security sap our sense of dependence on God, to remember the early days of struggle and simplicity. The prophets were constantly calling their people to 'return to the wilderness' (Hosea 2:14). The great spiritual revivals of the past sprang from this—the Desert Fathers (such as St Anthony), St Benedict and St Francis. Today perhaps, in a different kind of desert, Mother Teresa.

Finally, a note on finance

1. The priests were fed by the meat and bread of certain sacrifices (Leviticus 6:14–17).
2. People made freewill offerings (Exodus 25:1–5).
3. A half shekel was collected for temple upkeep. But it was also a thank offering for atonement (Exodus 30:11–16) which is why it was a poll tax. Jesus paid this under protest (Matthew 17:24–27). Atonement is a free gift.
4. Tithes—a tenth of the income from the land. One tithe was to maintain the Levites, our ministry (Numbers 18:21). Another was to pay for the sacrifices and feasts (Deuteronomy 14:22–26). A third tithe, collected only once in three years, was for the landless poor. Jesus supported the tithes but attacked their legalism. The giving he commended was both sacrificial and freely offered (Matthew 23:23–24; Luke 21:1–4).

Laws relating to secular life

Duty to the neighbour

In comparison with the laws of all other nations of the time, the Mosaic Law is notable for its compassion. Lacking police forces and prisons, justice was mostly summary and local. God was seen to be more merciful than humans.

Exodus 21–23 and Leviticus 19 are worth detailed study. Note how Leviticus stresses that God's people must be holy because God is holy, and the repetition of 'I am the Lord'.

This law of holiness covered all sides of life and is mainly concerned with protection.

1. *Protection from violence.* The law of an eye for an eye (Exodus 21–24) was designed to limit retaliation, not encourage it (compare Genesis 4:24). It is practised in the Sharia Law of Iran and some other Muslim countries today.

   Cities of refuge were set up to provide sanctuary for those who, before trial and condemnation, fled personal revenge and death. Throughout the Middle Ages, churches were used as sanctuaries. Criminals were allowed to stay for a month, after which they had the choice of either surrendering to lawful authority, or of being safely escorted to the coast to exile. Churches have been used today to give sanctuary to immigrants fearing deportation. Though there is no legal sanction for this, the British Government has respected the sanctuary (Exodus 21:12–24; Deuteronomy 4:41–43).

2. *Protection of the weak.* The old are to be respected (Leviticus 19:32). Very relevant today! The widow and orphan are not to be exploited (Exodus 22:22–23). The resident alien is to be given equality of treatment (Exodus 22:21–29; Leviticus 19:33–34; 24:22). The last verse is especially relevant to the racial discrimination of our cities. The disabled too were protected (Leviticus 19:14). In those days such disablement was regarded as a punishment for sin. This was true even in Jesus' day, and in some places today too (John 9:1–3). The poor were protected in many ways. Usury was forbidden within the brotherhood of Israel, and loans were to be interest free. Pledged clothing, if essential for warmth, had to be returned at night (Exodus 22:25–27). The poor were protected in the courts, but so also were the rich (Exodus 23:6–8; Leviticus 19:15), a principle equally important in the Communist revolutionary state. Wages were to be promptly paid (Leviticus 19:13). How many small businesses today fail to survive because of delay or non-payment of bills?

   The poor were to be given economic support. Producers of essential goods were not to be so greedy for profit that the last corner of a field should be reaped. Gleanings were for the poor (Leviticus 19:9–10). Every seventh year the land was to lie fallow. In days before rotation of crops and use of fertilizers this was needed to allow the land to recover and prevent over-use. But the reason given was that anything it did naturally produce should be for the poor (Exodus 23:10–11). Still more important was the Year of Jubilee (Leviticus 25:8–17, 23–24). This ensured that no Israelite was permanently deprived by debt of his land, his home and possessions, or of his liberty. Had this law been obeyed, which it was not, there would have been no landless poor or inequality. Socialism would be unnecessary. The mortgage problem would be solved.

3. *Protection for loss.* There were laws of compensation. A thief restoring stolen goods had to restore double. An animal stolen and killed must be made up for, four to five times (Exodus 22:1–4; compare Luke 19:8). The law of a goring ox, known to be dangerous (Exodus 21:28–30), could well be applied to owners of Rottweilers today! People's reputations were also protected by a law of slander (Exodus 23:1; Leviticus 19:16).

Business dealings were to be honest (Leviticus 19:35–37). Practical help must be given to those in trouble, whether friend or foe (Exodus 23:4–5).

4. *Protection of health.* The priests were responsible for diagnosing leprosy. There were many other skin diseases that could be mistaken for it. Lacking other facilities cases had to be isolated (Leviticus 13–14). A law even covered sanitation (Deuteronomy 23:12–14). This is still relevant in many parts of the world today. Verse 14 might well apply to our litter, rubbish disposal and pollution!

5. *Protection of marriage.* The laws against marrying close relations (Leviticus 18) are, with some changes, still found in *The Book of Common Prayer*. Inbreeding can lead to weakness, sterility and insanity, as members of European royal families have discovered.

Divorce was permitted (Deuteronomy 24:1–3). Jesus said this was a concession to people's weakness (Mark 10:2–9). Homosexual practices were forbidden (Leviticus 18:22). To accept and have a compassionate understanding of people with such an orientation is Christian, but when it comes to sexual practice the New Testament is as strict as the Old (Romans 1:26–27). Christ did not condemn anyone, except the hypocritical and the self-righteous. But neither did he water down the high standards of the Law (Mark 10:1–12). In fact he raised them to cover thoughts and intentions.

6. *Protection from evil* (Exodus 22:18; Leviticus 19:20–28). While it is true that in the Middle Ages many innocent women were put to death, the recent repeal of the law against witchcraft has led to a mushrooming of covens and Satanist cults indulging in black magic, ritual abuse and murder. Dangerous occult practices penetrate even our schools. Occult books fill the shelves of books labelled religion. What begins as excitement ends in fear, addiction and death.

The Law was summed up by Jesus who quoted Deuteronomy 6:5 and Leviticus 19:18. It is to be interpreted not according to strict observance of the letter, but according to the Spirit of love.

The Book of Deuteronomy (Second Law) contains much repetition of the previous books, but it stresses the importance of obedience, with warnings of curses and promises of blessings.

The curses of chapter 28 should not be seen as retaliation by an angry God, though there may have been something of this in the mind of the writer, who lacked the knowledge we have of Christ. We can interpret them as the miserable consequences of sin. The licence of the egotist to do and get what he wants regardless of God or his neighbour enslaves and deprives others. It separates him from loving relationships and he ends up finding himself in bondage. These curses were used by the prophets to warn their people to repent of their sins, or they would be taken into captivity. They did not repent and, in captivity, they meditated on the prophets' warning. This led to a transformation taking place in their attitudes and way of life.

The Law is given as a blessing, not to bring us into bondage, but to preserve and train us for freedom. It was a school master to lead us to Christ (Galatians 3:24).

Deuteronomy confronts us with a stark choice. We know God's commandments. He speaks his word in our hearts. To say no is to choose evil and death. To say yes is to choose good and life (Deuteronomy 30:11–20). 'Therefore choose life.'

For further reading

Psalms 19; 119:1–40, 129–136; Matthew 5; Galatians 5:13–25

For group discussion

1. Does ritual help or hinder your worship?

2. Does your church encourage and use the creative arts?

3. Can modern investment become the sin of usury?

For private reflection

1. What does the priesthood of all believers mean to you?

2. Has the shape of a church building and the structure of its worship any spiritual value for you?

3. Should Christians tithe?

5

The Conquest of Canaan

Joshua; Judges

We now return to the story of Moses and his recalcitrant people. Slowly they learnt discipline. God's presence was with them in the cloud over the tabernacle. When it moved they moved. When it stopped they stayed (Exodus 40:34–38; Numbers 9:15–23). They learnt to be led.

At last the call to go forward sounded again, 'You have circled the mountain long enough.' Deuteronomy 2:2 is a wonderful challenge to us when we get stuck. Because of their fear and faithlessness the Israelites had been stuck in the desert for thirty-eight years (Deuteronomy 2:14). Now they move towards Canaan.

The first obstacle they met was Edom. The Edomites were descendants of Esau, and God told Israel they were not to fight or possess Edom. When the Edomites refused to allow them peaceful passage, the Israelites withdrew (Numbers 20:14–21; Deuteronomy 2:4–8). They withdrew to Mount Hor where Aaron died. Miriam had died earlier. Let us take leave of Aaron with the words of his blessing upon us (Numbers 6:24–26). His priestly office was transferred to his son and so to all descendants (Numbers 20:22–29).

The Israelites, bypassing Edom, came to the borders of Moab and Ammon. These were descendants of Lot, and their land too was protected (Deuteronomy 2:9, 19). Their battles were with Sihon, king of Heshbon, and Og, the giant king of Bashan (Deuteronomy 2:30–33; 3:1–5, 11). His land, a strip of territory just east of the river Jordan, was given to the tribes of Reuben and Gad. They accepted Moses' condition that they should share in the fighting for Canaan until all their brother tribes were also settled (Deuteronomy 3:15–20).

Although Moab was not attacked, the invasion of such a large successful force of immigrants frightened Balak the king of Moab. The story of how he hired the prophet Balaam to come and curse them is told in Numbers 22–24. In spite of God's prohibition, Balaam set out to meet Balak. The contradiction of 22:20 is the result of editors combining two versions of the story. An angel blocked his path. Balaam's ass with animal awareness was, unlike the prophet, sensitive to this unseen presence. It refused to budge. God sometimes has to get us into a tight squeeze before we get the point! Balaam gets the message, more likely through his guilty conscience than literally through the ass's mouth. God allowed him to proceed in order to bless instead of curse (Numbers 24:1–14). His blessing ended with the prophecy of a rising star, a sceptre of Israel. This pointed beyond the kingdom of David, to Christ (Revelation 22:16).

It was now time for Moses to hand over to a successor. He was led to choose Joshua, the name he had given to Hoshea (Numbers 13:16). It is the same name as Jesus, and means saviour.

Joshua was experienced in battle, and the vital part played in it by prayer (Exodus 17:10–13). He had gone up the mountain with Moses and shared in the vision and communion feast (Exodus 24:13). A man filled with the Spirit (Numbers 11:24–30), he was constantly in the presence of God (Exodus 33:11). He had been one of the scouts sent to spy out Canaan, and, with Caleb alone, had pleaded for the people to advance (Numbers 14:6–10). He was thus a man of action and a man of prayer.

Moses commissioned Joshua with the laying on of hands (Numbers 27:18–23). The charge he gave him is found in Deuteronomy 31:7–8.

Deuteronomy 32 contains the Song of Moses with its two beautiful images of God as the 'Rock' (verse 4) and the mother eagle (verse 11). Deuteronomy 33 records the blessing he gave to each tribe. It includes the much-loved and quoted verse 27, 'Underneath are the everlasting arms.'

Finally, Deuteronomy 34 describes Moses' ascent to the top of Mount Nebo with its panoramic view of the Promised Land. There he died, still vigorous. His grave is unknown. The greatest of all Israel's leaders, Moses prophesied that one greater than he would come (Deuteronomy 18:15–19). This may have been the starting point for Jesus' Bible study given while walking the road to Emmaus.

For further reading

Psalms 135; 136

The Book of Joshua

Taking over from a great man is never easy. There are bound to be comparisons. The new leader wonders, 'Am I up to the job?' Joshua needed encouragement if he was to have confidence. He also needed assured confirmation of his authority. God gives him both, in a command and a promise. Like Abraham and Moses before him, Joshua responds with obedience and faith (Joshua 1:1–9). The people too offer encouragement and support. Honeymoon periods are usual. Something more was needed. With bold faith Joshua leads them across Jordan on dry ground. It is just like the crossing of the Red Sea. After this Joshua's authority was unquestionable (chapters 3–4). A similar cutting off of the Jordan waters took place early in this century, caused by a rock fall. A rare natural event can become a miracle when human faith and God's perfect timing are brought together. Some have thought that the calm waters of the normally turbulent Channel crossing at the time of the Dunkirk evacuation of the British forces was such a miracle.

On the eve of the battle Joshua goes out alone to take stock of the city he had to take, and, no doubt, to pray (5:13). A man stands facing him with a drawn sword. Joshua challenges him, 'Are you for us or against us?' 'I am captain of God's army' is the reply. God is not on anyone's side. What matters is that we are on his. To Joshua this was an experience similar to Jacob's before his meeting with Esau, a divine encounter that must have changed his life.

He now knew exactly what he had to do. For seven days the army encircled the city in silence, the priests bearing the ark. Then, on the final round, they shouted, and the walls came 'tumbling down' (chapter 6).

Certainly the already demoralized citizens must have been terrified by all this and shattered by the shout. Was it a figure of speech or a miracle? Many have searched for explanations. Jericho is the oldest city known to us and the foundation of walls can be seen to be 9000 years old. But the archaeologists tell us these fell before the time of Joshua's arrival. We don't know exactly what happened. 'The walls fell flat and that was that.' The event has become legendary, and symbolic of walls of every kind that can be felled by faith (Hebrews 11:30; Psalm 18:27–29; 2 Corinthians 10:5). The Bible constantly teaches that battles are won by faith, not numbers or fire-power. Faith is more than morale, for through it God himself is actively at work. But faith depends upon a clear conscience. One man's cowardice can start a rout. In this case one man's disobedience lost the battle. All the people knew that the spoils of war belonged to God who gave the victory. But Achan stole some of it for himself (chapter 7).

To us the punishment seems harsh. Joshua's gentle words show personal compassion, but the crime was deeply serious. One lost battle could shatter morale, prove to their enemies that Israel was not invincible, and lose them the whole campaign. In those days families were accountable for crimes committed by their members. Achan's family had connived and not reported the theft. In our own society there is also now a move to make parents responsible for the crimes of their children.

Joshua too could make costly mistakes (chapter 9). He had instructions from Moses to make no treaty of peace with any Canaanite tribe

(Deuteronomy 7:2). Knowing this, the Gibeonites planned a trick. It worked. Joshua, like his men, trusted his own eyes and ears and believed their story. He failed to ask God for advice and made peace with them. It led to a lot of trouble in the future. At the time it led to Joshua having to defend them against a league of five Canaanite kings who gathered to wreak vengeance on these Gideonite 'traitors'. The league was decisively beaten at Makkedah, and this gave Joshua control of the south (10:3–8, 28).

One verse (Joshua 10:13) has created problems for those who take everything in the Bible literally. It is, as it says, a quotation from a book of poetry. Poetry expresses experience through imagery. Most of us have experienced a moment of crisis when time stands still.

Chapter 11 describes Joshua's northern campaign against Hazor, north of Galilee. He then defeats the Anakim, the much feared race of giants, who, from then onward, are confined to Gath and Gaza (Joshua 11:22; Numbers 13:33; 1 Samuel 17:4). This ends the records of Joshua's campaigns (Joshua 11:23).

The rest of the book describes the division of the land between the tribes. From then on they were responsible for completing the conquest of their own territory. This led to complaints and failures but Joshua took a strong line with such (17:13–18), refusing to bail them out. The tabernacle was set up at Shiloh, about twenty miles north of Jerusalem—which had not been conquered. The tribes of Reuben and Gad, their promises fulfilled, were allowed to return home (Joshua 22:1–6). Then it was Joshua's turn to bid farewell. He summoned the people and their leaders, and repeated to them the commands and warnings Moses had given in his farewell speech (Joshua 23). He called to them to renew the covenant. Again, like Moses, his voice rings out, 'Choose you this day whom ye will serve' (Joshua 24:15 AV). He will accept no superficial response. He records their promise of loyalty and obedience in a book, and sets up a stone of witness (24:14–27). Then Joshua sends the people home. His mission of breaking the power of the enemy, and opening up the Promised Land for his people has been finished (compare John 19:30) and this great precursor of Jesus dies. The book of Joshua ends with the burial of Joseph's bones at Shechem, the modern Nablus (24:32).

The Book of Judges

Our transition from the Book of Deuteronomy to that of Joshua has been as smooth as the transfer from Moses to his successor. In fact an important boundary has been crossed.

The Jews divided their Scripture into three classes: the Law (in Hebrew

Torah), the Prophets and the Writings. The Law consisted of the first five books, and was given supreme importance. Joshua, Judges and the books usually regarded as historical were classed with the Prophets.

Just as the opening chapters of Genesis are concerned with meaning and purpose rather than scientific origins, so the writers of these were less concerned about historical accuracy, for which they lacked sufficient records, than about interpretation. As they looked back over what they remembered of their long history they asked, 'What has God been saying to us through our experience?' In these books they are speaking out on behalf of God, which is what the word prophecy means. Many different authors have been at work, and as we have seen earlier three versions of the stories have been threaded together.

According to the Book of Joshua, the conquest of Canaan was speedy, and was seen as a series of extraordinary Acts of God. Entry into Canaan was as miraculous as the exodus from Egypt. The Book of Judges sees it differently, as a long drawn-out and hard struggle. There is truth in both versions.

Judges starts where Joshua ends, with the failure of the tribes to 'drive out' all the Canaanites. The repetition in Judges 1:19–20, 27–34 is emphatic. To the writer, looking back, this failure was the cause of all later troubles. The pure worship of Yahweh was contaminated by the idolatry of Canaanite worship, with its fertility cults. Particularly dangerous was the intermarriage with Canaanite women. It is often the women who pass on religion in the home.

There is now some evidence that Canaanite religion contained some insights that were valuable and which the Israelites may have absorbed to enrich their own beliefs. In the same way, the early Church found things they could learn from Greek philosophy, and we can sometimes hear God speaking to us through men and women of other faiths. There is a light God gives which 'enlightens every man' (John 1:9). We do not have a monopoly of truth. But we do have Jesus as a litmus test, a standard by which truth can be judged in other religions and our own. We also have the Holy Spirit to guide and keep us in the truth. Even so, our beliefs and lifestyle do get infected by those of the world around us.

The Old Testament writers knew of no such protection. They only saw the disastrous consequences of cultural and religious intermingling. As exiles in Babylon they believed God was punishing them for their people's infidelity. So Canaanites were seen as totally bad. To drive them out of the land was an act of obedience to God. At that time, under such circumstances, and with God's purpose in mind, dare we say that they were wrong?

These chapters in Judges also have importance in our world today. The Jews have returned, and are still returning to Palestine today, claiming that the land, given by God to their ancestors, was a permanent possession. They use these passages to justify the eviction of Palestinians, and their conflict with their Arab nations is a repeat performance of the wars with Midian, Edom and Moab, inheritors of the still older family feuds of Ishmael, Esau and Lot. In studying this book we handle material that could almost literally be radioactive! Some Christians take sides in the conflict. Those whose views of the Bible tend to literalism usually support the Jewish claim, though a few may reject it on the grounds of Jesus' parable of the vineyard (Matthew 21:40–41). Others may side with the Palestinians, partly because most Christians in Palestine, and there are quite a number, are Arab.

Over two thousand years have passed since the original conquest, and more than a thousand since it was recorded as it is today. God is still working out his purpose in our history today, but his ways are mysterious.

With all this in mind, let us now return to the text.

The book follows a clear and repeated pattern outlined in chapter 2. The Israelites believed that God was a God of the mountains and desert. He was a God of battles. But they now entered an agricultural land where the people believed good harvests depended upon the goodwill of the Baals. These were local fertility gods, whose worship was linked to human as well as animal sacrifice, and to ritual prostitution.

After the death of Joshua, and those who remembered his days and the covenant they had made with him, a new generation grew up that began to worship the Baals. Intermarriage with Canaanite women was a major factor in this (3:6–7). This separated them from God and from each other, and they were an easy prey for conquest. Each time this happened they repented and prayed to God for deliverance. In response God raised up judges who recalled them to faith and obedience, and led them into battle to defeat their enemy. After the judge's death the people would again relapse and the cycle of events would repeat.

Chapter 3 tells how Othniel delivered the Israelites from the king of Mesopotamia, and Ehud delivered them from the king of Moab. Neither is an inspiring story. But in chapters 4–5 we read about two most remarkable women.

Deborah was both a prophetess and a judge. In her time the Israelites were subject to Jabin, the Canaanite king of Hazor, who was powerfully armed with iron chariots. Deborah, in God's name, summoned Barak to take up arms. This he only agreed to do if she promised to go with him to battle. She agreed, but told him that God would give the honour of victory to a woman.

And so it was. Deborah led Barak up Mount Tabor, south of Galilee, and she gave the order for attack. The Canaanite army fled and was destroyed, partly by the flooding river. Its commander, Sisera, escaped, and took refuge in the tent of Heber, a Kenite, who had made peace with him. Moses' father-in-law was a Kenite (Judges 1:16) and the Israelites had always looked on Kenites as friends (Numbers 10:29–32; 1 Samuel 15:6). So they would have seen Heber as a traitor, which is obviously how he was seen by his own wife. Those squeamish of her methods might ask what others were available to a woman alone in a tent. Those who remember the joy and relief of Hitler's defeat and death will be able to identify with Deborah's song of joy (chapter 5). Together with Miriam's song (Exodus 15) it is one of the oldest records in the Bible.

Even more exciting is the story of Gideon and his battle with the Midianites (chapters 6 and 7).

Gideon's call came while threshing wheat, secretly, for fear of Midianite looters. An angel, a messenger of God, appears as it were in mufti. His greeting is the same as that with which Gabriel addressed Mary. Though Gideon is hardly acting like a 'mighty man of valour', the angel calls out his hidden qualities, which we see developing in the rest of the story.

Gideon's response is to question, 'Why all this trouble?' The angel's reply is a silent look. Gideon knows the answer (verses 7–10). Instead, the angel commissions him to deliver Israel himself. So often we are the answer to our prayer (Luke 10:2). But, like Moses, Gideon makes excuses. Expressions of humility are often a camouflage. When the call is repeated he asks for a sign. But, by this time, it isn't for the sort of sign an unbeliever asks to evade a challenge, but for a sign to confirm a believer who is ready to obey. Like Abraham, and like the disciples at Emmaus, it is as he makes an offering of food that he is given his sign, and an awareness of the presence of God.

God himself now takes command through an inner voice. Gideon is ordered to destroy Baal's altar and grove, and rebuild the altar of God. He has enough courage to obey, but only by night. Next morning, furious townsmen cry for his death. Gideon's father defends him and makes his own challenge to Baal. Gideon, now filled with the Spirit, blows the trumpet to rally the people for war.

As they gather Gideon again asks for a sign, which God gives, twice. At times, we all need to 'lay a fleece', to have our guidance confirmed. For now a far greater act of faith and daring is required. All the men who are fearful are told to go home. Out of twenty two thousand only ten thousand remain. A simple test, of battle alert perhaps, is set, and most of these are eliminated. Gideon is left with only three hundred men with which to face the host of Midian! He is encamped on a high ridge. God tells him to go down at night and spy out the Midianite morale. It is at an all-time low! The battle is won dramatically by a show of faith, a sudden burst of light, and trumpets sounding the charge. Without striking a blow, except against each other, the Midianites flee in terror and confusion. In the Second World War, General Wingate with his men, whom he called the Gideonites, expelled the Italians from Abyssinia by similar tactics, a combination of faith, scare tactics and bluff.

After various problems of jealousy with some of the tribes, Gideon was invited to be ruler. He refused. 'God is your ruler', he said. But he made one disastrous mistake. With some of the spoils of war he made an ephod, not a priestly garment as in Exodus 28:6, but some kind of religious emblem or image, that was later worshipped. No doubt he meant well, but breaking God's commandments is not the way to honour God. Notice how the Bible always records the mistakes and misdeeds of God's heroes, lest they should be given undue glory.

The story of Abimelech is a sordid one. Gideon had many wives and left behind him seventy sons. Abimelech was only the son of a concubine at Shechem. Thirsty for power, he asks his mother's people, 'Is it better to be ruled by seventy or one?' When they agree to support him, he takes money from a Baalite shrine, and uses it to enlist a band of hirelings. Then he goes and murders all his legitimate brothers, except the youngest, Jotham, who escapes (9:2–6). The men of Shechem then make Abimelech king. Jotham, standing on Mount Gerizim, the mount of blessing (Deuteronomy 11:29) uses a parable to curse both Abimelech and the men of Shechem. This is fulfilled by their mutual self-destruction. The men of Shechem revolt against their self-made king. Abimelech destroys both them and their city, and is himself killed by a woman throwing a millstone on him from the walls.

After two more judges, the dreary tale of idolatry and defeat continues. When the Israelites cry to God, his answer is, 'Let the gods you have chosen deliver you' (10:14).

The people turn to Jephthah. He is the son of a prostitute, thrown out by his family. How often God uses people whom others despise. The enemy is Ammon, whose land has been respected by Israel. But the Ammonites claimed the land of the Amorites which Israel had conquered. Jephthah challenges their claim (11:23–24). He regards his war against them as just.

Jephthah's successful campaign ended in tragedy as he is trapped by his foolish vow. It illustrates how far the practices of Baalism had infiltrated the minds even of these still loyal to God. To vow a child to God meant vowing him to the service of God (1 Samuel 1:12). God had shown Abraham that human sacrifice was unacceptable. The law provided for the cancelling of vows by minors and women, but not by responsible men. There was no way out.

After this tragic aftermath, jealous strife broke out with the Ephraimites, who could be distinguished by their faulty pronunciation. This explains how we get the word Shibboleth!

The next judge of note was Samson. Like so many leaders he was the promised son of a barren woman. His parents' experience with an angel was similar to that of Gideon (13:15–23). The woman showed more sense than her husband. The Bible describes many such women. Samson grew up to be a Nazarite, sworn never to drink or cut his hair. The secret of his phenomenal strength lay in keeping this vow.

The enemies of his time were the Philistines, who had invaded from the western sea and occupied what is now the Gaza strip. Then they controlled most of the land, thanks to their exclusive possession of iron weapons. Samson's destiny was to begin the work of his people's deliverance.

But Samson was lustful, self-willed and irresponsible. God sometimes works through very strange people!

Twice Samson married Philistine women, who infatuated and deceived him. The first wrested from him the secret of his riddle (14:17) and the second, the notorious Delilah, the secret of his strength (16:15–17). This led to its loss. He was blinded and enslaved. In utter wretchedness, stripped of all but God, slowly, as his hair grew, his strength returned. Then, brought into the hall of feasting, where the leaders of the Philistines made sport of him, he brought down the pillars and the roof on top of them. After a lifetime of frivolous campaigns (for example 15:3–8) Samson finally accomplishes his mission in life by sacrificing his own. Like Charles I, 'Nothing in his life became him like the leaving it'. Strangely, in this one point, even Samson can be seen as a precursor of Christ!

The rest of the Book of Judges is taken up with the sorry tale of Micah and the Danites (chapters 17 and 18) and the even nastier story of the Levite and the Gibeonites, that led to a war of the tribes against the tribe of Benjamin.

You can skip these chapters without loss. Their content is summed up, as is the whole book, by the last verse. Judges 21:25 is a diagnosis of the troubles that were past, and a pointer to the remedy lying ahead.

For further reading

Psalms 44:1–8; 115

For group discussion

1. Without common beliefs a nation falls apart. What beliefs hold ours together?

2. How can a prosperous society rediscover faith?

3. What justifies a people's claim to land? Is God involved?

For private reflection

1. Have you ever 'laid a fleece'? When is it faith and when is it superstition?

2. What walls need to be overthrown by prayer today?

3. Is your church over-concerned with numbers?

6

The Kingdom is Set Up

1 Samuel

Judges is followed by the Book of Ruth. It is a charming story about the great-grandmother of King David. It comes as a clean breath of air after the sordid fumes of Judges' closing chapters. Ruth however, belongs to that part of the Scriptures classed as the Writings, and, though set historically in the period just preceding 1 Samuel, it belongs to a very much later age.

The best thing perhaps is to enjoy reading it now, without comment, and perhaps write down what you think it is about. Then, when the book is discussed in the penultimate chapter, you will be able to compare what it said to you, and what it was designed to say to its first readers. Bible stories are open to many interpretations and God speaks his living word to us in many ways.

We have reached a period, about 1000BC. Much of the record is now based on contemporary accounts. The events are presented with detail. The characters are drawn in depth and the conflict between them makes a fascinating psychological study. It is their relationships with God however, that are central.

Samuel was the last of the judges, and the first great prophet since Moses. The story of his childhood is told in chapters 1–3. He, too, was the promised and longed-for son of a barren woman. Mary, the mother of Jesus, must have known Hannah's song of joy, for her own is full of its echoes.

Dedicated to God at birth, Samuel grew up at the shrine at Shiloh, as servant to Eli the old high priest. Eli had two sons who acted both as priests and judges. They abused their position and were a couple of scoundrels. Eli's weak reproofs were ignored. Eli, as father, was held responsible for their crimes.

(1 Samuel 2:25 raises the same problems and can be understood in the same way as Exodus 4:21.) God warned Eli, and at the same time gave him a promise that God would raise up a 'faithful priest' (2:35) which clearly points to Christ. The beautiful story of how Samuel came to a personal knowledge of God is given in chapter 3. God gave another

warning to Eli. It took courage for the child to deliver it. As Samuel grew he became increasingly aware that God was speaking to him, and soon all the people recognized him as a prophet.

We don't know how many years passed before the judgment on Eli's sons took place, but we do know the occasion.

At that time the main enemies of Israel were the Philistines. The Israelites, preparing for battle, decided to take the ark of God with them, probably against the wishes of Eli (chapter 4). Here was 'God in a box', a source of vain confidence to the Israelites, and terror to the Philistines. But God was never 'in a box'. After the rout of the Israelites and the capture of the ark, Phineas' widow called her son Ichabod. But the glory had departed before the battle had begun. God is not a trump card we can play to win our tricks. He plays the hand! Did Eli die because he had turned the ark into an idol?

To the Philistines the ark was an embarrassment. To their god it was a disaster. Chapters 6 and 7 tell how they came to return the ark. God certainly made his presence felt by his people's enemies!

Twenty years passed and Samuel was now an adult. He made his headquarters at Mizpah, and called the people there to meet him. He told them to renounce their idolatry and to fast and pray. As he was praying for them and offering sacrifice, the Philistines attacked. Aided by a violent thunderstorm, the Israelites defeated them. Samuel raised the stone 'Ebenezer' as a perpetual witness that the living God had helped them in the past. He would therefore not fail in the future as long as they remained faithful to him.

From then on Samuel acted as judge in Israel, and there was peace. But, like Eli, he too had trouble with his sons. Why is it that so often the sons of good men reject their fathers' ways? In many Eastern lands today it is because, unlike their sisters, they are spoilt. Sometimes religious leaders feel duty-bound to put their church duties first, and so neglect their families.

The people feared that, after Samuel's death, his sons would take over, and the land would again relapse into anarchy. They demanded a king who would lead them in battle and provide an undisputed succession. The following narrative reflects the ambivalence of the Biblical writers to this. Looking back over their history, they could see both evil and good in the monarchy. The first view is that the demand for a king was bad. It was a rejection of God (8:6–22; 10:17–25; 12:1–25). They were not to be like other nations. In times of need God had always raised up leaders of his own choice to turn them back to him. A hereditary king would become arrogant, and serve his own interest rather than God's. He would oppress his people and enslave them. The people continue to demand their own way, and God gives it to them—as he is apt to, and lets us suffer the

65

consequences (Psalm 106:14–15). Saul is chosen by lot, and Samuel seeks to mitigate the evil by writing in a book the principles upon which the kingdom was to be founded.

Here is the first example of limited monarchy. King and people are equally under the Law. There is a contract made between them. This made the Israelite monarchy unique and was to have profound importance for their history and ours.

The second view was that kingship is good. It is found in 9:1—10:6; 10:26—11:15. Saul is chosen by divine guidance. He is a man of humility, consecrated by holy oil and filled with the Spirit, for him an ecstatic experience. Those who rejected him are dubbed 'men of Belial'. After Saul has proved his ability to lead, his followers demand these men's death but Saul spares them. Under Samuel's leadership the kingdom is given a new beginning. With this view, the king is the 'Lord's anointed' and rules by divine right, a model Charles I was to follow. Power needs restraint. In the Old Testament it was the prophets who exercised this control.

Samuel now plans to retire. Whatever may have been the misdeeds of his sons, the people admit that Samuel himself was without reproach. He reviews their past history and disloyalty to God. Whatever the rights and wrongs of the matter, they now have a king. The basic choice is the same as that declared by Moses and Joshua, to serve God and be true to their calling, or to rebel and suffer the consequences. Note Samuel's promise of continuing prayer for them, 12:23.

To fail in this is seen as a sin against God. His final word is to tell them always 'to consider what great things God has done for you'. A study of Psalm 77 shows how this is a source of comfort in sorrow and perplexity, and of faith and hope in times of despair.

The rejection of Saul   *1 Samuel 13–15*

The next three chapters tell of three acts of self-will which led to the rejection of Saul as king.

The first (13:1–6) started with a skirmish against a Philistine garrison, led by Jonathan, Saul's son. This provoked a large punitive raid which terrified the Israelites, who had no iron weapons (13:19–20). Many started to desert and hide in the rocky caves. Samuel had promised to come and offer sacrifice before the battle began. He said he would come within seven days. On the seventh day Samuel still hadn't come. Seeing more and more of his men deserting, Saul decided to offer the sacrifice himself, though, not being a Levite, it was against the Law for him to do so. Just as the sacrificial ritual ended, Samuel arrived, still within the time promised. He rebuked Saul and warned him that, because of his faithlessness, God would give the kingdom to another.

God often tests our faith by stretching us to the point of no return, and saving us at the eleventh hour. He did this with Abraham on Mount Moriah. He did it again and again with Moses, and with Joshua and Gideon. Their faith never faltered. Saul wasn't in their league! Jesus was led beyond the point of no return, through total darkness to death. Salvation lay in resurrection, after defeat and death had been accepted and endured.

The next occasion was also sparked off by Jonathan's courage (14:1–46). He attacked a hill garrison after climbing a rock face regarded as unscalable. The lookout never expected their jeering invitation would be accepted. The surprise attack, coupled with an earthquake, led to total confusion, and the Philistines started fighting each other.

The Israelites were so heartened that the deserters returned, and even the traitors, who had joined the Philistines, came back. Once again, Saul tried to win God's favour by a self-determined religious fast, enforced with a curse. Not knowing this, Jonathan had eaten some wild honey. When he heard about it, he blamed his father for acting foolishly. Saul's victorious army was so starving hungry, that, after the battle, they seized the captured animals and ate them, blood and all (Leviticus 19:26). Saul tried to save the situation, but when he asked a priest to seek guidance from God, God was silent. Instead of blaming himself for the sin, Saul allowed all the blame to fall on Jonathan. He would even have killed him had not the army protected Jonathan. He had been the hero of the day.

Saul's third and most serious failure came after a battle with the Amalakites. He had been told to destroy everything Amalakite, both man and beast. To us this sounds horrific, but it was common practice in those days. In any case, the animals would have been killed to provide a sacrificial feast, which is why Saul spared the best of them. As for Agag, he would be expected to pay handsomely for his life and freedom, or was Saul, like Elizabeth I, reluctant to set an example of cutting off crowned heads? It seems that Agag, with his army destroyed and his power and reputation lost, no longer valued either life or liberty (15:32).

Like Achan, Saul was stealing the profits of victory that were not his by an act of disobedience. When Samuel arrives Saul puts on a mask of virtue, first with a lie, then, typically, with shifting the blame. Samuel's reply is a classic summary of the teaching of all the later prophets (15:22–23). Witchcraft! Yes, for witchcraft aims at controlling powers that belong to God. In disobeying God, we, like Adam, assert our own claim to ultimate sovereignty.

The final parting of king and prophet is intensely moving and dramatic. Note Samuel's courtesy in continuing to honour Saul in front of his men. How much he loved and grieved for him (16:1).

David is anointed and meets Saul   *1 Samuel 16–17*

How long Samuel mourned we don't know. God summoned him to go and anoint a new king, from among the sons of Jesse. At the risk of his life, Samuel goes to Bethlehem, and calls the people there to a sacrifice.

To his surprise, the sons of Jesse are rejected by God, one by one. 'The Lord seeth not as man seeth.' Once again, it is the youngest who is chosen. David is so disregarded by his family he wasn't even there. Now, all had to wait until he came, and there, in front of his family, Samuel anointed him. From that moment the Spirit of God came upon him, blessing him and filling him with wisdom. At the same time the Spirit left Saul, who became tormented by a spirit of fear and jealousy, leading to outbursts of rage and madness.

Then come two accounts of Saul's meeting with David, both deeply moving and ironic. The first tells of David being chosen as a harpist and singer who soothed Saul with his music (16:15–23). The other tells how David killed Goliath in single combat, using only a shepherd's sling as a catapult and a few carefully chosen stones.

The reintroduction of David's family (17:12–14) shows the separateness of the source, and the reference to David's fame as a fighter (16:18; 17:15) seeks to connect it with the other. Note how David's brothers still deride him, and David's question, 'What have I now done?' (17:29), which hints at a long experience of criticism, is a question he continually repeats as he meets the hostility of Saul.

Saul tries to arm David with his own weapons. But it is Saul's trust in his own strength that has been leading him to disaster. David rejects them. He is safely wrapped in the armour of God, confident faith and a single-minded regard for God's honour (17:45–47). This sums up the difference between the two men.

Both accounts give a truthful picture of David, and both show the mutual attraction of the two men. Far from recognizing David as his hated supplanter, Saul loves him, and makes him a member of his own household.

Growing Jealousy   *1 Samuel 18–20*

This ideal situation did not last. God's Spirit, enhancing David's natural charm, made him enormously attractive. His friendship with Jonathan, Saul's son, has become proverbial. His restrained behaviour won him the loyal support of Saul's army officers, his seniors in age and experience over whom he was promoted. Michal, Saul's younger daughter, fell in love with him.

It was the songs of the women at a victory celebration that aroused

Saul's jealousy to such a pitch of mad rage that he attempted murder. David's double miraculous escape, and his wise discretion, led Saul both to suspect and fear him.

From then on David walked on very thin ice. He learnt to experience the guidance and protection of the Lord as his shepherd, which freed him from fear (Psalm 23:4). What was Saul to do with a rival, so universally beloved, who never put a foot wrong?

Saul began to set traps for David, but David did not fall into them. His anointing was a secret between him and God. His family would not dare to speak of it. Those free of personal ambition cannot be corrupted. As Saul's fear grows he becomes increasingly dangerous. Jonathan pleads for David in vain. Michal covers his escape from the palace and saves him from another attempted murder. Saul sends soldiers after him. They find him with Samuel at what reads like a charismatic meeting and return empty handed. The story of Saul's similar experience may have been added as an alternative explanation of a familiar proverb (1 Samuel 10:10–11).

David arranged to meet Jonathan secretly. Jonathan made one last attempt to speak for David. Furiously rebuked, he echoes David's question (20:31–32) and is nearly murdered himself. He returns to David, and, after making a pact of eternal peace, the two friends part.

Saul's war against David and the Philistines *1 Samuel 21–25*

David first fled to Nob, where he persuaded Abimelech, the priest, to give him the shewbread—bread offered to God as food (21:1–9; compare Matthew 12:1–4). He was also given Goliath's sword, and then fled to Gath with it! The king of Gath, seeing him as Saul's enemy, and so perhaps a valiant ally, received him with favour. His army however, already recognized David as Israel's *de facto* king! (21:11). Only a pretence of madness got David out of that situation alive.

He then found refuge in the cave of Adullam and the rocky heights by the Dead Sea. Here he lived like a brigand chief becoming a rallying point for all discontents. David's family was under threat, as were all Bethlehemites. He managed to persuade the king of Moab to give refuge to his parents, but he could not protect Abimelech. Saul's horrific revenge and overkill reflected the extent of his mad fear (22:6–23). David heard of it from Abiathar, Abimelech's one surviving son. It was a burden of grief for him. Abiathar stayed with him and became one of his most loyal priests.

If Saul complained of ingratitude, David had greater cause. After asking God about it, he led his followers to rescue the town of Keilah from the Philistines. But God warned him it wasn't safe to stay there. Saul planned to besiege it and the men of Keilah would certainly hand David over for the sake of peace. Note how important it was for David to have Abiathar with the ephod, which was used as a means of discovering God's will and guidance in any situation (23:9–12).

Apart from a brief lull caused by the need to fight the Philistines, Saul spent the rest of his life seeking and chasing David round the mountains.

What agony of divided loyalty Jonathan must have suffered. He stayed with his father to the end, but somehow he managed to slip away and meet David in a wood. Here he 'strengthened David's hand in the Lord'— a lovely phrase, and told him that both he and his father knew that David would succeed to Saul's throne. With this Jonathan at least was content.

Two stories are told of how David spared Saul's life. To him Saul was 'the Lord's anointed', whom to harm would be a great sin (24:6; 26:11). To prove to Saul that he could have done so, in one case he cuts off the hem of Saul's robe, and, in the other, takes his spear and water bottle. In both stories Saul repents and proclaims his love for David. 'Thou art more righteous than I' (24:17). He acknowledges what Jonathan has already made known about David and the succession. In spite of this, David wisely does not trust him, and stays safely in the mountains.

Chapter 25 tells how David came by his wife, Abigail. Saul had given Michal as wife to someone else. Forced to live like a brigand, David had either to ask for supplies of food or fight for them. He sent to Nabal, whose name means fool, asking very politely for some provision. He gets a very rude reply and plans to attack and seize it for himself. Nabal's wife is a sensible woman. Hearing of David's courteous request, the peaceful, even protective behaviour of his men, and the contemptuous refusal of her husband, she anticipates David's reaction. Her prompt, generous response is warmly appreciated. David is thankful that he has been saved from taking revenge. Nabal however, when he recovers from a drunken bout, is shocked into having a stroke which kills him. Abigail shows no inclination to mourn for him. She is happy to go and become David's wife.

David and the Philistines   *1 Samuel 27; 29–30*

This is probably another much more detailed version of David's visit to Gath briefly given in 1 Samuel 21:10–15. In this story Achish, king of Gath, not only believes David is an enemy of Saul, and so a valiant ally, he also gives him the town of Ziglag. David takes this opportunity to attack Israel's old enemy the Amalekites. When Achish questions him he demonstrates his loyalty to Achish by a lie, saying that it was the Israelites he had attacked. An alliance of Philistine kings was preparing for a major battle with Saul. Understandably, they did not trust David and told Achish to remove him from military command. One wonders what David would have done if he had been forced into battle. This time his question, 'What have I done?' (1 Samuel 29:8) might have been rephrased and given back to him, 'What are you going to do?'

David returned to Ziglag to find that the Amalekites had taken their revenge, burning the city and taking the women and children captive. David, who had thus lost two of his wives, wept with his men. Then he pursued the Amalekites, defeated them, and rescued their captives. There were two important outcomes of all this. First, David established the principle, ever afterwards followed, that those who stayed to guard the camp should have equal rights with those who fought. The second was that David used his share of the booty to send as presents to the elders of Judah, who had shown him friendship when he had visited them in his time of need.

Saul's end   *1 Samuel 28; 31*

The Law punished witchcraft with death (Exodus 22:18) and forbade the consulting of mediums (Leviticus 19:31). Saul, in his earlier days, had enforced the Law. Now, half-crazed with fear, as he sees the Philistine host approaching, he disguises himself, and seeks out a witch who still remained in hiding. He forces her to call up Samuel, hoping Samuel would give him reassurance and advice. As Samuel appears, the medium realizes that her visitor is Saul. Saul calms her fears, but Samuel doesn't calm his. Samuel tells him that God is no longer with him. The kingdom belongs to David. Saul and his sons will suffer defeat and death.

Many Christians today, who have had experience of mediums, would deny that a holy man like Samuel could be conjured up. They say that evil spirits masquerade as the people called for by a medium. These use their occult knowledge to deceive and usually provide seemingly comforting, though banal messages. Their aim is to draw people's hearts away from trusting dependence on God. Such an evil spirit would delight in reducing Saul to despair.

So Saul's last battle was joined. He and three of his sons, including Jonathan, were killed. Only the courage of men he had saved in his first act as king (1 Samuel 11:1–13) rescued their bodies from final humiliation and gave them burial.

The story of Saul and David is the most movingly dramatic of all Old Testament stories. From one view point Saul can be seen as a typical tragic hero, destroyed by a fatal flaw, jealousy. It destroyed him and made him a destroyer (compare Genesis 4:5–8; Matthew 27:18).

What had David done? It is clear what he had not done. Though anointed to be king, David never pushed at the door of opportunity, or tried to make a bid for power. Saul, his jealousy once aroused, could read crafty ambition into everything David did. Was his wisdom that of the Spirit, or of the snake in the grass? To a clouded mind the difference is not apparent. We judge others from our knowledge of ourselves. Is anyone innocent of mixed motives? Our actions spring from our overriding motive. For David this was loyalty to God. On this depended his loyalty to Saul.

The reason why the biblical writers gave so much importance to this story was that it illustrates the two views of kingship. Is it the king who rules, or God? From a worldly point of view Saul was a good king, a strong leader, who combined religious devotion with practical common sense. But God's strength and wisdom is greater than human common sense (compare Isaiah 55:8–9). His choice of a slave race, and of younger sons, illustrates the belief that the purpose for Israel was greater than a worldly one. It is beautifully expressed in Isaiah 49:3. For this reason, David, for all his faults, was the ideal king.

For further reading

Psalms 18; 23; 31

For group discussion

1. List the virtues and faults of Saul and David and compare them.

2. What qualities did Jonathan need to remain loyal both to his father and his friend?

3. Has the rule of God any meaning in a democracy?

For private reflection

1. How did you first hear God speaking to you? In what other ways does he speak?

2. How can we judge whether or not our motives are good? Can we rightly judge those of other people?

3. Are there people with whom we have had a quarrel for whom we should be praying?

7

The Glory of the Kingdom

2 Samuel 1; 1 Kings 1–11

The kingship of David   *2 Samuel 1; 1 Kings 1:1—2:11*

David becomes king   2 Samuel 1:1—5:5

The news of Saul's death was brought by an Amalekite. He claimed to
have finished off Saul at Saul's request. He brought with him Saul's crown,
obviously expecting David to rejoice at his news, and reward him for the
crown. David did neither. He mourned for Saul, and had the man
executed. Diplomacy or genuine feeling? His lament (2 Samuel 1:19–
27) rings true and is deeply moving. King James' version brings out its
poetic beauty.

David was now proclaimed king at Hebron, but only by his own tribe,
that of Judah. Abner proclaimed Ishbosheth, Saul's surviving son, and
was given the support of all the other tribes. The split that eventually led
to the division of the two kingdoms started here.

The result was a civil war. It was embittered by a personal vendetta
pursued by Joab, David's captain, against Abner, who had, very unwil-
lingly, killed Joab's youngest brother.

The war went on seven and a half years. Then Abner had a quarrel with
Ishbosheth, and went to visit David. He offered to bring over to David all
the ten tribes, including Benjamin, the tribe of Saul. David agreed to such
a peace and Abner went and talked round the elders of the tribes. He then
brought them to David who feasted them. After this he was sent off in
peace to bring over the tribes.

Joab had been absent during all this. When he heard about it he was
furious. Without David's knowledge he called Abner to a meeting. Abner,
trusting in David's peace, went and was murdered.

This rash act could have alienated the tribes and restarted the war, had
it not been for David's strong reaction. He disclaimed responsibility,
cursed Joab and mourned for Abner. The people believed in his sincerity
and approved.

Later, Joab accused David of loving his enemies more than his friends. David had mourned for Saul and Abner. Next he mourned for Ishbosheth. Two of Ishbosheth's captains murdered him, and reported this to David. They too expected him to be pleased. Instead, David reminded them of the fate of the Amalekite, and had them also put to death.

This repeated public demonstration of respect for Saul's family and army captain won over the tribes, and David was anointed king of Israel.

The city and the house of David   5:4—7:29

David now had to make his throne secure from Israel's enemies. His first act was to capture the walled city of Zion, Jerusalem, and make it his capital. He then had to defeat the Philistines who, hearing he had been made king of Israel, came to attack him. Remembering how he had been sheltered by, and taken service under the king of Gath, they had added reason for hostility and their determination to bring him to heel. As always, David took his battle orders from God, and was victorious.

His next move was to bring the ark into his new city. Ever since its return by the Philistines, it had been in Gibeah. The sudden death of Uzziah, while trying to steady the ark from falling off the ox cart in transit, may have been due to a heart attack. The ark, covered in gold, with its golden cherubims, would have been a tremendous weight. But the priests interpreted his death as God's punishment for sacrilege. David was both angry with God and frightened. He decided to let the ark stay put.

We don't know which of the Psalms David may have written, but one of their refreshing characteristics is the way they freely express anger with God, and lay bare all feelings, bad as well as good.

The ark however, proved to bring such a blessing that David again decided to bring it to his city, where he had prepared a tent for it. It was brought with great joy, and David, stripping off his robes, joined in the dancing and singing, regardless of his dignity as king. Michal was disgusted. David had demanded her return, but she left her second husband reluctantly (3:13–16). Her resentment now turned to sarcastic contempt. This was not the way for royals to behave. Brought up as a princess, she should know! But David remembered his shepherd origins. He would never stand on his dignity before God. He never lost his simplicity. From then on it seems that Michal was his wife only in name.

To David, glory belonged only to God. He had built a fine house for himself of cedar brought from Lebanon (5:11–12). He wanted to build a fine house for the ark, more worthy of God's honour. The prophet Nathan encouraged him. Then God told him to tell David not to do it. God did not want a house. He preferred the tent.

The priestly Chronicler gives a more priestly explanation (1 Chroni-

74

cles 28:2–3). David, as a man of war with blood on his hands, is not worthy of so holy a task. As with the kingdom, so with the temple, the biblical writers are ambivalent. The conflict of their views has continued to the present day.

Does God need a special house? Solomon, in his prayer at the dedication of the temple, acknowledges that he does not. At his trial on the charge of attacking the temple, Stephen quotes both Solomon and Isaiah (Isaiah 66:1–2; Acts 7:47–51). God is everywhere. He has no rest on earth. In cloud and pillar he is ever on the move. However, today as then, we need holy places as a focus for our worship, and places where we can meet for prayer. But populations move. Buildings are static. In our work and witness we are bogged down by their expense and inflexibility. The church building can become more important than God!

To return to the story of David, it was not David's plan to build a house for God that mattered, but God's plan for building a house for him. God promised David a son who would not just build the temple, but would rule over a kingdom which should be established for ever. In part this promise was fulfilled by Solomon, but its complete fulfilment was in Christ (Luke 1:32; Mark 10:47; John 19:19; Revelation 11:15).

David's sin   2 Samuel 11–12

Chapters 8 and 10 deal with David's wars. Helped by the loyalty and skill of Joab, his commander, David defeated all the surrounding nations. Moab, Syria, Ammon, Edom, Amalek, as well as the Philistines, all were overcome. Chapter 9 tells how David looked for any surviving member of Saul's family to whom he could show kindness. Mephibosheth was found, a son of Jonathan, who was lame. David handed over to him all Saul's land and possessions, and invited him to take his meals in David's palace.

We have seen how the Bible always records the weaknesses and sins of its heroes. David sinned on two occasions. The first began with an act of adultery.

It was the season for war and David's army was away fighting. But David 'tarried' in Jerusalem. If he had been with his men he wouldn't have got into trouble. Instead he was relaxing and enjoying physical comfort. He was off guard, a suitable time for the devil to attack.

The adultery was sin. Worse were the efforts made to pin the responsibility for the child conceived upon Uriah. Did Uriah suspect David's motive? Certainly the reason he gave for refusing to go home was a rebuke to David. Worst of all was the plotting of Uriah's death. This was murder. David was only acting like the kings of all the nations he had been fighting. But David was not like them, and God did not turn a blind eye to his sin.

Nathan handled his difficult commission with great skill. His story not only appealed to David's sense of justice and compassion, but woke memories of his shepherd days. David gives his verdict, and then, with a shock, hears the accusation: 'Thou art the man.'

How differently David now behaves from other kings. He confesses his sin and repents. He prays, not for himself, but for his child. When the child dies he accepts the loss without complaint, and concentrates on consoling the mother. The result was the conception of Solomon. David, who bore no resentment against Nathan, sends him news of Solomon's birth, and Nathan gives the child another name, Jedediah, 'Beloved of the Lord'. David's sin had been very great, but, because of his humility, the experience, far from alienating him, drew him closer to God. Out of it God brought blessing. The terrible events, however, that God had revealed to Nathan about David's family, cast a shadow over the future.

David and Absalom   2 Samuel 13–19

The disaster developed slowly. Its root cause was David's failure to discipline his sons. In this he was like Eli and Samuel. In chapters 13–15 we read the sordid story of Tamar's rape by her half-brother Ammon. Absalom, her full brother, boils with anger but bides his time. David knows, but does nothing. The explosive situation goes on simmering for two years. Why? Was David too busy, or too besotted with Bathsheba and Solomon, to deal with it? It's easier to turn a blind eye and hope that time will quieten things down. Anything would be better than a family row with a spoilt and favourite son. David doesn't accept Absalom's invitation to the sheep-shearing feast, and is reluctant to let Ammon go. Did he suspect there might be trouble? Jonadab, his nephew, knew that Absalom, ever since Tamar's rape, had been planning murder. After the murder David wept, but his mourning for Ammon did not last long. His real mourning was for the fugitive and exiled murderer. Joab, seeing how David yearned for Absalom's return, took a leaf out of Nathan's book. He found a way for David to allow Absalom to come back to Jerusalem without personally receiving him. Absalom isn't satisfied with this, and, when Joab refuses to give him any further help, he takes petulant revenge by setting Joab's barley field on fire. Joab, though angry, sees the king on his behalf and Absalom is allowed into the royal presence. David gives him the kiss of peace. All is apparently forgiven, but no word of repentance is heard. On either side! For no doubt Absalom blamed David for not executing justice on Ammon himself.

The situation, left unhealed, grew worse. Handsome, popular, his head turned with praise, Absalom's ambition grows. He plans to usurp the throne. Justice was done at the city gate. There the king would sit to settle the disputes of any who came to him. But David, in his old age, gets neglectful, and Absalom takes his father's place. After winning popular favour, he makes a lying excuse and goes to Hebron. There he conspires to rally Israel to his support, a deliberate reopening and exploiting of the rift between the tribes which David had tried so hard to heal! In sorrow and humiliation David is seen at his best. His thought is all for others. He leaves Jerusalem, not to save his life, but to save the city. He tries to release Ittai from any sense of duty in following him. He utterly refuses to allow Zadok the priest to carry the ark out of the city.

Brokenhearted and in tears, he climbs the Mount of Olives bare-footed. There he hears of the defection of Ahithophel, his closest counsellor. No curse, not even a word of reproach comes from his lips, only a prayer that God would not allow Absalom to benefit from Ahithophel's wisdom.

Blow follows blow. Mephibosheth, Saul's crippled son, whom David had treated so kindly, is rejoicing over the situation. He has the ridiculous hope that Absalom will let him be made king. Then, as David continues his journey, Shimei, a relative of Saul, showers curses and stones upon him. David takes it all quietly, as a rebuke from God. Did he ever get over his sense of guilt for being, in some way, responsible for Saul's death?

Absalom enters Jerusalem, and, to show that he is now effectively king, fulfils Nathan's prophecy. Thanks to Hushai, Ahithophel's wise advice to attack David immediately is not taken. David is given time to muster his army. God had answered his prayer. His situation was saved. Joab leads David's army into battle and is victorious. But David had ordered that no harm should come to Absalom. This order Joab immediately disobeyed. How dramatically told is the story of how David hears of Absalom's death. How terrible is his grief and deep his mourning. How understandable is Joab's rebuke: 'You love your enemies and hate your friends' (19:6). In David's eyes Joab was no longer a friend. He would never trust him again.

The aftermath   2 Samuel 19:20—24:25

Joab was soon given further cause for his reproach. The Israelites had fled, but David was not sure of the loyalty of the men of Judah. Several had left Jerusalem and followed Absalom to Hebron (15:11). When Absalom had entered Jerusalem in force, he had given command to Amasa, a cousin of Joab. So David sent a message to Zadok and Abiathar, his faithful priests, to contact Amasa. They were to offer him Joab's position as David's commander, if he would secure for him the loyalty of Judah. Amasa agreed, and David was invited to return to the city.

Rats reboard a ship that is refloated. As David returns, Shimei comes to him pleading for pardon. David grants him his life. Mephibosheth also comes crawling with a poor excuse for his disloyalty, and is given back half a share in his inheritance. The Israelites, with Absalom dead, now seek a way of returning to David, and quarrel unsuccessfully for the privilege of escorting him home! How fragile was their loyalty! Sheba, a Benjamite, rallies them again to battle with a cry for independence. David orders Amasa to nip this new danger in the bud, but Amasa delays, unwilling to advance against the men he had so recently led. So David calls on Joab's brother to go after him and take over command. Joab goes too, smarting with anger, and, overtaking the unwary Amasa, kills him as, years before, he had killed Abner. He then goes on, with his brother, to make an end of Sheba. From then on it is Joab who is again David's commander, but the jealousy between the men of Judah and the northern tribes of Israel remained.

Another running sore, hindering peace, was the anger of the Gibeonites. These were the people who, as a result of trickery, had been given a solemn covenant of peace by Joshua. Saul had repudiated this, and no peace was possible without reparation being made. They refused to be paid off with gold. Life must be given for life. To secure peace David sacrifices seven members of Saul's family. He saved Mephibosheth, Jonathan's son, but gave up Michal's sons by her other husband. After their death he gave them, and Saul and Jonathan, honourable burial in their family tomb.

David made one last attempt to fight the Philistines, but he was forced to recognize his age and the political importance of his safety. Gracefully he steps down. In the following battles the last of the giants of Gath were killed.

The 'might of Israel' could no longer fight, but the sweet singer could still sing. The psalm in chapter 22 is, with minor variants, the same as Psalm 18. In the cave of Adullam David would certainly come to think of God as the Rock of his salvation. Note the repetition of 'my'. It was a very personal experience. The psalm recorded in 1 Chronicles 16 is a combination of Psalms 105:1–15; 96:6–9; 98; 136 and 106:47–48. David may not have written these psalms himself. A reference to the temple (2 Samuel 22:7) makes it unlikely. But they certainly reflect his anguished cries and joyful faith.

David gave the Levites, led by Asaph, a ministry of praise. Their songs were accompanied by all kinds of instruments and frequently dancing. Such joyful variety of expression is now being reintroduced into the sober and conventional worship of some of our churches. 2 Samuel 23 lists David's mighty men. The story of how they brought him water from the well of Bethlehem, and his reaction to their heroism, is typical. He pours it out as a sacrifice to God.

About this time David organized a census of his fighting men (chapter 24). To us this would seem to be a normal and sensible thing to do. To the biblical writers it was a much more serious sin than his adultery. None knew better than David that battles are won by faith, not numbers. He overrode Joab's opposition, but, when a prophet challenged him, David confessed his sin. A widespread outbreak of what may have been plague was accepted as God's punishment. It is certainly true that the sin of a ruler can bring disaster to his people. History is littered with examples.

What is wonderful is that the finding of a suitable home for the ark is linked to the ending of the plague. The angel of destruction sheaths his sword standing by the threshing floor of Araunah. The incident not only recalls the night of the Passover, it points back to the sacrifice of Isaac, for, by tradition, this is the summit of Mount Moriah. Here at the very place where God promised to provide a lamb, the temple was built. On it now stands the Dome of the Rock. Calvary is less than a furlong away. Araunah offers the site free of charge. David's reaction is typical. His words to us ring out over the centuries (24:24).

David and the succession   1 Kings 1:1—2:11

David had promised Bathsheba that Solomon should succeed him as king, but like many rulers he put off confirming the succession. It was bound to create problems. Postponement led to trouble. Another son, Adonijah, tried to seize the throne with the support of Joab and even Abiathar the priest.

Thanks to Nathan the prophet, Zadok the chief priest, and David's mighty men, the plot was foiled. With David's authority they anointed Solomon king, and sat him on David's throne. Adonijah's supporters fled, and Adonijah sought sanctuary. Solomon agreed to spare his life, and received his homage.

David's last concern was to rally support for Solomon, still a very young man, and hand over to him the plans and materials he had been collecting for the temple, which Solomon was to build. Details are given in 1 Chronicles 28–29. It must be confessed that David also gave Solomon the task of punishing Shimei and the faithful Joab. This was not only wise advice in the interest of continuing peace and unity between the tribes, it also reflects the very serious view taken by David on covenant breaking. It was a sin not just against God. It was a sin against the blood of the victim. It was a breaking of the third commandment. Because of this, David handed over Saul's relatives to the Gibeonites. Because of his covenant with Jonathan he refused to hand over Mephibosheth. Joab had twice broken a covenant of peace by an act of murder.

David's final pledge and blessing is given in 1 Chronicles 29:10–20. 'Thine, O Lord is the greatness, the power and the glory.' These wonderful words of praise form part of the offertory prayer in the Anglican Communion Service. For all his faults, David was the ideal king, ever loyal, ever humble, ever trusting. God came first in his life. Joab accused him of loving his enemies. Peace and unity is what David sought for his kingdom with constant singleness of purpose. Christ both loved and died for his enemies. Servant and Son of God, he was also the promised son and heir to David's everlasting kingdom.

The kingship of Solomon   1 Kings 1–12

In David we reach the high point of the monarchy. In Solomon we cross its watershed.

Securing the succession   1 Kings 1–4

Solomon's first task was to secure his succession. Adonijah clung to the altar, and Solomon respected the claim to sanctuary and gave him conditional pardon. This was cancelled when Adonijah asked permission to marry the Shunammite woman, who had looked after David in his old age (1 Kings 1:1–4). She was the beloved of Solomon round whom the great love song 'Song of Solomon' was written (Song of Solomon 1:1–2; 3:11; 6:13). Solomon's deepest emotions were aroused as well as his feelings of insecurity. So Adonijah was executed. Abiathar the priest was merely dismissed. Joab too claimed sanctuary, but Solomon rejected it. Joab himself had twice broken covenants of peace. Shimei agreed to confinement in Jerusalem. His visit to Gath gave Solomon grounds for executing him, as convincing as Shimei's pretext, if not more so! Adonijah had claimed to have the support of Israel's ten tribes, so Solomon's position was precarious. He was young and inexperienced. In his dream Solomon asks God for wisdom. The very next morning proof is given that this was granted. There were no witnesses to support the claim of either prostitute. Solomon's judgment has become legendary. It is used as a climax to Brecht's play *The Caucasian Chalk Circle*. Wisdom, a gift of God's Spirit, is recognized as residing in Solomon, and made his throne secure.

David's wars had also left the kingdom secure. Years of peace, and control of the main trade routes, brought prosperity and great wealth. God's promise to give Solomon the riches he had not asked for was fulfilled. Both the wisdom and the wealth of Solomon are proverbial.

Solomon's temple   1 Kings 5:1—9:9; Psalm 132

These things receive less full treatment from the biblical writers than the building of the temple. To this four chapters are devoted. The building took seven years. Note however, that the building of his own house took nearly twice as long (6:37—7:1). The ark was brought into the temple and placed behind the veil as described in Exodus. Men and women can raise buildings, but only God can fill them with his presence. When this happened, so overwhelming was the cloud of glory that the priests couldn't go on with their duties. They could only fall flat on their faces in worship. Today great revivals have started when similar events have taken place.

Solomon's prayer at the dedication shows that the temple is a focus. God dwells in heaven unlimited by time or space. But his eye is on the temple. His name is there. God's people don't need to come to the temple. It is enough if they turn towards it (compare Daniel 6:10), even if only in thought.

God is both transcendent—out there, beyond me—as well as imminent—here, within me. It isn't easy to keep these two aspects in balance. A focus of attention can be helpful. It could be a cross, an icon, or a candle. Jesus referred to himself as a temple (John 2:19). In this sense he is an icon of God. We, as members of his body, are also called to be icons of God, a focus of his presence, for others!

The king kneels to pray. Power is corrupting, and is seen at its most terrible in the hands of those who either have no God to kneel to, or who identify God with themselves. In all his glory, Solomon kneels, both in his heart, and visibly in front of all his people. Then he rises to bless them. He calls them to remember all God has done for them, to be obedient, not just to secure blessing for themselves, but to bring blessing to the world. This takes us back to Abraham.

1 Kings 8:60 reflects the faith of the writer. Only after the exile were the Jews convinced that no other Gods existed, though there may have been flashes of dawning insight beforehand. This verse expresses the glorious conviction of Second Isaiah (Isaiah 45:18, 21–22). It is because the writers were inspired to interpret past events that we, similarly inspired, are enabled to see their relevance for us today.

Power and glory   1 Kings 9:10—10:29

After twenty years Solomon was at the height of his power and glory. He built cities to house great storehouses and his thousands of horses and chariots. He built a navy. He accumulated huge quantities of gold and exotic luxuries from Africa.

He was also credited with writing three thousand proverbs. Though the books of Wisdom belong to a much later age, Solomon probably introduced a class of moral teachers, wisdom scribes, and was patron to them and to a large group of historical and court recorders, musicians and the like.

His fame spread far and wide. The Queen of Sheba came to see if all she heard was true. It was. It was understated. She was awed and astonished, and returned home, so it is believed, pregnant with Solomon's son, from whom the kings of Ethiopia—Lions of Judah—

claim descent. When Mengistu toppled the emperor and seized the palace, he kept the lion he found there!

All this glory belonged to Solomon. It is a far cry from the words of the Chronicler, put into the mouth of David (1 Chronicles 29:11). Solomon was leading the nation in a wrong direction. Israel's vocation was not worldly power but servanthood. Their God was to be their glory (Isaiah 60:19).

Seeds of trouble   1 Kings 11

Beneath all the wealth and power, trouble was brewing. First there was heavy taxation and forced labour. Though one version of the story says only non-Israelites were involved in such labour, another indicates that Israelites too were conscripted (1 Kings 9:21–23; compare 5:13–18).

There was also the requisition of supplies needed to feed a large retinue and maintain the court in a lifestyle as extravagant as that of the former Romanian dictator, Ceaucescu (4:26–28).

The other trouble stemmed from Solomon's foreign wives. They demanded not just their own houses, but shrines for their gods. Solomon planned such marriages to secure political alliances. He probably never imagined that his love of these women would lead him to being seduced into sharing their worship. God won't play second fiddle either to political expediency or sex. Twice God warned Solomon, but Solomon didn't listen. God warned him that because of his disloyalty all but one tribe would be disloyal to his successor, and would split away, dividing the kingdom.

Does God punish? The biblical writers were sure that he did. We are squeamish about this. One reason is that we know God is love. But loving parents discipline their children (Hebrews 12:6–11). Children who can get away with anything are unhappy and insecure. Increasingly violent behaviour is often a search for secure boundaries. Parents who ignore this, or who utter meaningless threats, are despised. The other objection is that God can't or won't interfere. This isn't open to secular standards of proof. But actions do have consequences. There are also coincidences, and our conscience leads us to make connections. It is dangerous however, to make such connections in regard to others as happened when lightning struck York Minster! The biblical writer looked back with eyes of faith to read the judgment of history.

Solomon already had two enemies inherited from his father: Hadad, an Edomite, with a base in Egypt, and Rezon of Syria. Israel's enemies have not changed over the years! The most dangerous enemy was Jeroboam from Ephratha, another name for Bethlehem. He was a man of courage and ability whom Solomon had put in charge of forced labourers. Jeroboam is confronted by a prophet from Shiloh, once the sanctuary for the ark, who prophesies that God will make Jeroboam king of the ten tribes. Here is prophecy as foretelling joined to prophecy as forthtelling God's purposes. It is also self-fulfilling, as Solomon foresaw. Somehow he got to hear of it, and tried to kill Jeroboam, who had to flee. How ironic! Solomon was now replaying the role of Saul in the conflict with his own father, David.

These dangers simmered, but Solomon himself was unassailable.

For further reading

Psalms 21; 45; Proverbs 3; 8; Matthew 4:8–10; 6:27–30

For group discussion

1. Is Joab's criticism of David inevitably flung at any would-be peace-maker involved in the conflict?

2. Do we need special church buildings? How can they best be used?

3. How should Christian parents discipline their children?

For private reflection

1. What images do the words 'power' and 'glory' bring to your mind? How has Christ transformed them?

2. Do we expect God to play second fiddle in our lives? If so, to what?

3. Can dancing be a form of worship?

8

Division and Decline

1 Kings 12–22; 2 Kings 1–15

The kingdom splits   1 Kings 12:1–24

The moment for which Jeroboam had been waiting had arrived. Hardly were the royal burial rites over when a message recalls him to lead the Israelites in a confrontation with the heir.

What a dramatic scene! Jeroboam interrupts the coronation preparations, and, backed by an angry vociferous crowd, he demands redress of grievances.

Rehoboam, like Absalom, is arrogant. Brought up in Solomon's palace, he sees royalty in terms of privilege and absolute power. He ignores the advice of older, experienced counsellors, and encouraged by his arrogant friends, he returns a harsh answer. The result is the cry, 'To your tents, O Israel!' The enraged Israelites marched out of Rehoboam's presence and set up Jeroboam as their king (note Proverbs 15:1–2; 16:16–18).

Rehoboam's instinct was to fight, but a prophet stops him. This thing is of God. God's hand is seen in the fulfilment of prophecy. It is also seen when wrong policies lead to disaster. When this is recognized the disaster can become a point of growth. But the lesson takes a long time to learn.

The great sin   1 Kings 12:25—13:34

Rehoboam was not able to win back the ten tribes by fighting. What might win them back was the temple. Unity was only to be found in God.

Ever since coming into Canaan the greatest danger had been the seduction of Baal worship 'upon the hills, and under every green tree' (Deuteronomy 12:2). It was to check idolatrous worship that the law forbade all sacrifices except those offered at the temple in Jerusalem. So the temple was Rehoboam's trump card and Jeroboam had good cause to fear its power of attraction.

So he built two altar shrines, north and south of the country. The golden calves he installed in them were not Baals, but only images of

84

God. But what memories they would evoke! It was a flagrant breaking of the second commandment. A further scandal was to create a new priesthood from the 'lowest of the people'. No doubt the 'better class' would refuse to be involved in such unauthorized ordination. Worship offered to God in disobedience would find no favour. Like rulers all through history, Jeroboam was using religion for political ends.

Right from the beginning, prophets condemned these altars. Jeroboam replied with threats and attempted bribery. Both failed.

The story that follows is hard to understand. A prophet, who bravely rebuked Jeroboam for disobedience, on his way home, is punished for his own. Trusting the word of a fellow prophet he acted without consulting God, just as Joshua had done, when making peace with the Gibeonites. Our instinct is to cry 'It isn't fair. The punishment was out of all proportion to the mistake.' But the story remains, an awesome warning that those who preach to others, must themselves practise what they preach. A vicar convicted of adultery will suffer far more than a parishioner guilty of the same offence. Fair? Possibly not. Fact, certainly.

Judah was also unfaithful. Shrines on the high places contained images, and sodomy was practised. In our permissive society it now receives, together with other sexual practices, a toleration not countenanced by Scripture (14:23–24). Judah was attacked by Egypt, who stole the temple's golden treasures. Continual war was waged with Israel, and Judah found itself fighting on two fronts.

Chapters 15 and 16 make dismal reading. The temple was further depleted when its silver treasures were sent to Syria as a political sweetener. Wars and murders abounded. Reigns were short. Omri, who reigned over Israel many years, and achieved great political success, is passed over in four paragraphs. It is interesting to wonder, how much of what is in our own history books might be dismissed by the biblical writers as unworthy of record. If we shared their values, how might we rewrite them?

Elijah and Ahab   *1 Kings 16:29—21:29*

In 1 Kings 16:29 we meet Ahab, a weak king with a notoriously evil and strong-minded wife, Jezebel. If several chapters are devoted to his reign, it is only because of his conflict with Elijah, regarded as the greatest of the prophets. In the next three chapters his dramatic story is told.

Jezebel led Ahab into the active promotion of Baal worship. Elijah confronted him and prophesied a drought. Forced by Jezebel's threat to flee to the land of Sidon, he is cared for by a widow, whose son he raises from the dead, by combining the prayer of faith with the kiss of life. After three years, he returns to confront Ahab again. Note the wonderful thumbnail sketch of poor, faithful Obadiah!

On Mount Carmel a dramatic confrontation takes place with the priests of Baal. God proves to be no extinct volcano! Fire from heaven falls. Then the boy sees a distant cloud, no bigger than a man's hand. Elijah warns the king to drive home with all speed, or he'll be washed away! His faith is justified. Rain also falls in torrents, and Elijah, filled with the Spirit, runs before Ahab's chariot all the way to Jezreel, about forty miles! Even allowing for exaggeration, it was a marathon run by a marathon man.

Elijah's success is short-lived. Jezebel swears she'll have his head, and again he has to flee. He falls into a deep depression and wants to die. So often, times of spiritual exultation are followed by times of failure and despair. The swing of the pendulum is too much to take. Self-confidence is broken.

How wonderfully God restores Elijah. Note the stages of his restoration. First his exhausted body is restored. Tender loving care, in the form of food and drink, is provided, with nothing to do but sleep. Then comes the journey, not more running, but a long walk, through wilderness. It is a pilgrimage, back along the track leading to Sinai, the mount of God, back to the roots of faith, the rock of vision.

There, standing where Moses had stood (Exodus 33:21–23), Elijah meets with God. God questions him, 'What are you doing here?' Elijah had come to complain. How good that he could do so openly to God, and express even his death wish. There is no rebuke, only a command to stand and wait for the vision. Wind, fire, and earthquake, symbols of elemental power, shake the mountain. But God is in the still small voice. Here is power, greater than all the powers of earth.

The final restoration comes as God gives Elijah three practical things to go and do. These will alter the political landscape, and provide him with a successor. Elijah thought he was alone. He is not. Seven thousand faithful Israelites remain. Experience of Russia has shown us that even seventy years of persecution and atheist propaganda has failed to stamp out faith, which quietly smouldered on in countless hearts.

Elijah, in fact, only fulfilled one of his three commissions. He called Elisha, who carried out the other two for him. But first, the centre of interest returns to Ahab, who is attacked by Syria. The point of this story, told in chapter 20, lies in verse 28. God was seen by the Syrians as a god of mountains, of winds and storms. This is why the Syrians planned to fight on the plains. God sends a prophet to Ahab to tell him to fight on the plain, for God will prove his sovereignty there. Today we marginalize God in other ways. He is God of religion, and God of the Church, but holds no sway in the realm of politics, or economics, in business or leisure activities. We are called to go into battle, declaring his sovereignty everywhere.

The close connection between the God of Israel and social justice is seen in the story of Naboth's vineyard.

Jezebel, as a princess of Tyre, would have a very different view of kingship to that of Ahab. Kings of Tyre had an absolute right to do whatever they liked. Baals were not concerned with what today is sometimes scornfully called 'bourgeois morality'.

Ahab covets Naboth's land. When his generous offer to buy it is refused, he sulks like a child, but he never thinks of challenging Naboth's right. Jezebel takes control of the situation. She sets up a judicial murder. Ahab asks no questions, and makes no protest, though he must have guessed his wife's involvement. Satisfied that his own hands are clean, he goes to take possession of the vineyard. Here, he is again confronted by Elijah.

'Hast thou found me, O mine enemy?' Ahab is found, caught red-handed. Sentence is pronounced. Ahab, a weak rather than a bad man, repents and is personally spared. One is left wondering how Jezebel would react to the sackcloth!

No tame prophet: Ahab and Micaiah   *1 Kings 22*

War with Syria continued, and Ahab took the opportunity of a visit from Jehoshaphet, king of Judah, to seek his help in regaining lost territory. Jehoshaphet was a good king, and had ended the long fratricidal war with Israel. Jehoshaphet agreed to help, but only if God was consulted. Ahab lined up his tame prophets, who predictably prophesied victory. Jehoshaphet was not taken in.

'Is there not here a prophet of the Lord besides...?' There is, but he had not been summoned. God's prophets are not tame. Micaiah is called, and warned to toe the line. This he parrots so obviously that Ahab is driven to command him to speak the truth he does not wish to hear. Micaiah prophesies defeat and death in a most provocative manner. In reward he gets a smack on the head from the leader of the other prophets, and a prison sentence from the king.

In wartime, all governments tend to claim that God is on their side. They try to tame the Church to toe the acceptable line, especially if the Church is established as a state Church. This is why they seek to control the appointment of Church leaders and, in some countries, the staff of theological colleges. In such places Christians have had to set up underground counter-systems of training.

Ahab hoped to escape the fulfilment of Micaiah's prophesy. He resorts to a cowardly stratagem, and goes into battle in disguise, leaving his ally to fight in royal robes. The Syrians start to target Jehoshaphet, but, recognizing him in time, leave him alone. Ahab is killed by the random arrow of a nameless bowman. So God frustrates human stratagems! The cost of being a true prophet is great: prison, labour camp, psychiatric hospital or even murder. But the cost of silencing truth has to be paid by governments, and that also can be great. Truth will eventually out and dictators fall.

Fire from heaven   *2 Kings 1*

What are we to make of this story? Azariah, Ahab's son and successor, falls ill and sends messages to consult Beelzebub, god of Ekron about his recovery. Elijah intercepts them with the question, 'Is there not a God in Israel?' He tells them to take God's message back to the king, that the king will die. And so he does. So much is clear. But what of the three bands of soldiers sent against Elijah, on whom he calls down fire from heaven?

Stories grow up around all great men. The lives of saints are full of true events interwoven with legend. The spectacular event on Mount Carmel would have given Elijah an awesome reputation. The fire he called down from heaven to vindicate the sovereignty of God, now is used repeatedly for self-defence. Rather a come-down! We are sorry for the poor soldiers.

But behind the legends of hagiography, there is a strand of truth which points to the character of the saint. Fire is a symbol of spiritual power, and of God's Holy Spirit. More than any other Old Testament prophet, Elijah was a man of spiritual power. Such power can quell an attacking crowd. Jesus passed through the crowd at Nazareth which was intent on throwing him over the precipice. John Wesley passed through a similar murderous crowd at Bristol. So did my own great-grandfather, when vicar of St George's-in-the-East, at the time of the riots connected with the Tractarian movement in 1859. But fire from heaven, while burning up evil, is a fire of love. It glorifies God, but doesn't destroy men. Jesus did not permit James and John to call it down to destroy the inhospitable Samaritans. The corrupt use of spiritual power is the devil's work (Luke 9:54–56).

Elijah's passing   *2 Kings 2:1–18*

A mystery surrounds the passing of Elijah. It recalls the cryptic reference to Enoch (Genesis 5:24). It was believed Elijah never died, but was taken up to God in a whirlwind. No-one saw this except Elisha, and Elijah's experience, as recorded, bears a resemblance to the ascension of Jesus.

The emphasis of the story however, is on Elisha. He knows his master's end is near. Despite discouragement, he sticks to him like glue, following him from place to place, never letting him out of his sight.

When Elijah asks him what he wants, he asks for a double portion of Elijah's spirit. This will be granted if he sees Elijah's passing. What he saw affected his whole life: chariots and horses of fire, that carried Elijah away. His awareness of the constant presence of those chariots freed him from fear. Later, in a situation similar to that of Elijah in the previous chapter, he prays for his servant to see them too (2 Kings 6:15–17). Jesus also was aware of this army of angelic protection, but he chose not to call upon it (Matthew 26:53–54).

Elisha picked up the mantle that Elijah let fall, and used it to divide the waters as Elijah had done. Inheriting the mantle is now proverbial. How important also is the parting of the waters as the first step in spiritual responsibility. Moses at the Reed (or Red) Sea, Joshua at Jordan, now Elijah and Elisha, make this an act of faith in the sovereign and, to us, miraculous power of God. The mantle, without the faith to use it, provides no genuine authority.

Stories about Elisha   *2 Kings 2:19—8:6*

The following chapters tell stories connected with Elisha. Some, like the stories of the widow and her pot of oil, and the Shunammite woman and her son, are very like stories told about Elijah. The summons to advise the king of Israel in his war with Moab recalls the summons of Micaiah by Ahab, only Elisha's prophesy is favourable. It is interesting that, in this case, Elisha used music perhaps to send him into a visionary trance. Elisha performed many miracles. His fame in this respect was noised abroad. He was known as a healer, as in the story of Naaman, (chapter 5) and as a clairvoyant (6:11–12). His healing powers extended to the healing of the waters (2:19–22) (compare Moses, Exodus 15:24–25) and a pot of poisoned food (4:38–41). It might be possible to offer some scientific explanation of these two miracles, but not of the rescue of the axe head by making it float (6:1–7). Of special interest is the feeding of the hundred men, (4:42–44) which foreshadows the miracles of Jesus.

Newtonian physics discounted the possibility of such miracles, but the splitting of the atom, and the discoveries of Einstein and the new physics, have undermined the basis for such assurance of unbelief. The signs and wonders associated with the charismatic renewal have shown that, in the context of faith, God can and does do things beyond our understanding. But, where faith is absent, not even Jesus can work miracles (Mark 6:5–6).

The only discordant story is that of Elisha cursing the children. There were at least forty-two of them, and their description could apply to eleven-year-olds. We know, only too well, in our inner cities today, how frightening such a crowd can be, especially to someone they catch alone.

Elisha is not frightened. He is angry. Balding young, he may well have been sensitive on this subject. But to jeer at God's servants is to jeer at God, a serious sin at any age.

As with the lion and the prophet (1 Kings 13), the connection with the bears may have been coincidental. But curses do have power, and Elisha lived in a harsh pre-Christian age. In these days of renewal of spiritual power, we need to be aware of the dangers, not just of the occult powers of non-Christians, but of demonic influence in Christian leaders. As we have seen, Jesus was aware of this danger to his own disciples (compare Matthew 16:23; Luke 9:52–55).

For Elisha, healing was something that applied to the whole of life. We see this in the stories of Namaan, and the blinding of the Syrian army (6:8–23).

The Israelite maid, captured by the Syrians in a raid, could easily have hated her captors. But Namaan and his wife must have been kind, for her heart was healed, and she cared about Namaan's healing. The king of Syria's letter was taken by the king of Israel as a provocation for war. Elisha, knowing all about it, tells him to send Namaan to him.

Namaan goes expecting a prophetic display of miraculous fireworks. All he gets is instruction, by a servant, to go and bathe in the Jordan, a muddy stream in comparison to the Tigris and Euphrates. First Namaan's pride has to be healed. Then, through an act of faith and obedience, his body is also healed. Lastly, his spirit. He returns to Elisha, humble and grateful, and declares his faith in Israel's God. His request for a load of earth is due to the belief that gods are attached to the soil of their people. He asks pardon for the necessary outward performance of rituals in the Temple of Rimmon as part of his official duties. It is a situation familiar to many secret Christians in Hindu society today. Elisha would have denounced such compromises in an Israelite. He sends Namaan home with peace, but the greed and lies of Gehazi are exposed, and meet with appropriate punishment. We are judged by the use we make of our freedom, and our knowledge and experience of God.

We have already looked at the story told in chapter 6 as an illustration of Elisha's clairvoyance, and his awareness of the protection of the chariots of fire. Would that we all could have our eyes opened, like those of the young man! We have also seen how stories told about Elisha are similar to stories told of Elijah. But note the difference here. Instead of calling down fire from heaven to destroy the soldiers, Elisha calls on God to close their eyes, so that they fail to recognize that the way he takes them is going in the wrong direction towards Samaria. Elisha will not allow the king to kill them. Instead he sees they are fed, and then sent home. This generosity led to a healing of the political situation. At least for a time, the Syrian raids stopped.

The peace didn't last. The Syrian army returned to besiege the city, and there was terrible famine. Biblical writers tend to denounce kings of Israel, especially the family of Ahab, because of their compromise with idolatry. But not all were bad, and Jehoram was one of the best (2 Kings 3:1–2). He suffered with his people and under his royal robes, he wore sackcloth. Horrified by his discovery of cannibalism in the city, he turned his anger on Elisha. He blamed him for saving Syrian soldiers from death, and their commander from leprosy. He threatened Elisha with death, as Jezebel had threatened Elijah.

Elisha had still not fulfilled God's command to anoint other men as kings of Syria and Israel. He may have been waiting for a sign to show him the right time for such drastic political action. Now, he felt, the time was ripe. But first God tells him to prophesy a miraculous end to the famine. Elisha obeys, and is disbelieved. Four lepers, escaping from the city, find the Syrian camp deserted by soldiers but stocked with food. They returned to tell an incredulous king. The city is saved, and the prophesy is fulfilled. The writer of the story, typically, uses the fatal stampede as an opportunity to moralize on the sin of unbelief.

Elisha then travels to Damascus. The Syrian king, who had a high regard for the prophet, sends Hazael to him with a gift, to ask if he will recover from his sickness. Hazael is the man Elisha was told to make king. He tells Hazael that the king will surely die, but not from his sickness. Rigid with shock because of what, perhaps through clairvoyant insight, God has shown him, Elisha breaks down and weeps. Although he knows the consequence will be horrific, he still is faithful to his commission. He tells Hazael that he will be king of Syria, and warns him of the evil he will then commit. The result, as Elisha had foreseen, was political murder.

As predicted, Hazael revives the war with Israel. Like his father Ahab, Joram calls in help from Judah, now ruled by Ahaziah, whose mother was Jezebel's daughter. Both states were now ruled by the descendants of Jezebel, who was still alive, exercising her evil power behind the two thrones.

Joram, badly wounded in battle, goes to Jezebel's home in Jezreel to recover. Ahaziah goes there too, to visit his uncle. Here is a dangerous ganging together of the clan.

Elisha now sends one of the prophets' sons, with a box of consecrating oil, to Jehu's army headquarters. There, following Elisha's instructions, he secretly anoints him. Jehu, supported by his men, rides to Jezreel at a furious pace, now proverbial. Both kings and Jezebel meet their death. Naboth is revenged, and Elijah's prophesy is fulfilled.

Here is a mystery. Why does God use a greater evil to punish evil (Habakkuk 1:13)? Both Hazael and Jehu were more violent and cruel than the men they killed. Jehu went on to massacre the whole of Ahab's family. Ahaziah's mother, Athaliah, in self-defence, seized power, after murdering all her grandchildren. One, however, Joash, the youngest, was saved by the priests, who hid him in the temple. Athaliah was able to reign for seven years. Then the priests organized a palace revolution. Athaliah was killed and the child Joash (also called Jehoash) was crowned king. He grew up devoted to God, and his reign became a time of great reform.

The writers of the Books of Kings and Chronicles were able to accept all the horrors performed by Jehu without any sense of horror. He killed all the prophets of Baal, but the deceitful strategy he used fills us with disgust. How could the Chronicler attribute his massacres to God?

All through history Christians, too, have justified appalling cruelty by claiming God's approval. The Crusades, the fires of the Inquisition, the mutual slaughter of Catholics and Protestants, have sickened people, and turned them against religion. The Old Testament writers at least did not have the teaching and example of Jesus to show them a better way. For them was there a better way? Is there for us today?

Years after the event, the prophet Hosea denounced the murders of Jehu, and prophesied that they would lead to the final downfall of the kings of Israel (Hosea 1:4). He looked forward to a cleansing of the nation through suffering. Such an experience would prepare them for a different kind of king (Hosea 1:10–11).

Descent into chaos   2 Kings 12–15

Slowly, in both kingdoms, things went from bad to worse.

In Judah, the bad was a frustration of hopes. Jehoash—or Joash as he came to be known, so as not to be confused with Jehoash king of Israel—decided to repair the temple. The priests were told to collect money, but no repairs were done. Did they hoard it or pocket it? The king told them to stop collecting, and a huge collecting chest was placed at the entrance to the temple. As it filled up, the money was removed under the supervision of the king's secretary, melted down, and then given to the builders and carpenters. The job progressed, but a threatened attack by Hazael was bought off by the gift of most of the gold from the temple treasury. It was a shortsighted policy. Danegeld always tempts the aggressor to return for more!

Joash's efforts at reform led to his being murdered by his own servants. His son, Amaziah, brought up to respect the Law, took only limited vengeance, and then embarked on a foolish policy of aggression. After defeating Edom and annexing a city there, he then challenged Israel. Ignoring the king's warning, he attacked and was defeated. He was escorted back to his own city as a prisoner. He had to hand over all that remained of value, both in the temple and in his palace, as well as hostages. Finally, he too was plotted against, and murdered.

In Israel the situation was worse. After his murders Jehu reigned for twenty-eight years, then his son reigned for seventeen. After that Jehoash succeeded. During his reign Elisha died, and Jehoash wept. Elisha was like a chariot of fire to him, and, in his wars with Syria, he needed such a chariot. Even in death Elisha worked miracles!

Jehoash died of natural causes, and so did his son Jeroboam II, who reigned forty-one years. He set about a policy of conquest more successfully than Amaziah, and even conquered Damascus. The writer notes that Damascus rightfully belonged to Judah. David had conquered it (2 Samuel 8:5–6). God was left out of account. Only politics and grabbing territory mattered. The consequence was just. The army took over. Kings were murdered in rapid succession by army captains, who seized the throne, and were murdered in like manner in their turn. Life for royals was, to quote Hobbes, 'nasty, brutish, and short'. Chaos reigned.

But, over the dark mystery of returning chaos, the Spirit still broods, giving hope of re-creation.

For further reading

Psalm 34; Mark 9:1–13; 15:34–36

For group discussion

1. How do governments today try to use the Church for political ends?

2. Should religious leaders be judged more harshly than ordinary church members?

3. Do miracles happen today? Can you witness to or describe any?

For private reflection

1. What can we learn from Elijah's experience about how to comfort others?

2. Does the protection of angels mean anything to you?

3. How do we marginalize God?

9

Prophetic Protest in Israel

Amos; Hosea

Before true hope could revive God's people, false hope had to be dashed. The need above all was national repentance, a return to God and obedience to his laws. Israel had been called to a high vocation as a witness to God, and an instrument of his plan of salvation for the world. This vision was lost. There was little to distinguish the kingdoms from their neighbours, except their prophets. In those dark days God raised up a number of great men. There had always been prophets in Israel, and though the professional prophets were mainly sycophantic and bogus, there were, as we have read, others who were truly inspired.

These new prophets whose books bear their names, though they did not write them, had much in common with the earlier prophets. But there were differences. They were not, by and large, given to working miracles, though they did have dreams and visions. They had a passionate concern for social and economic justice, and a disgust for religious observance divorced from public and private morality, such as singing 'hallelujah' in church on Sunday and cheating your neighbour or going off with his wife on Monday! They looked beyond the petty politics of quarrelsome kings, and saw, in the advance of great imperial armies, the imminent judgment of God.

Their message was similar, but their personalities and experience widely different. The first of these prophets was Amos.

An angry shepherd   *Amos*

We know little about Amos except his name, where and when he lived, and his occupation. He was a sheep farmer who also had fig trees, and he lived in Tekoa, about fifteen miles south of Jerusalem. He prophesied in Israel during the reign of Jeroboam II.

Amos probably went up to Bethel, just north of the border, to sell his wool and figs. It was one of the two cities where Jeroboam had installed calves and made centres of worship. What Amos saw appalled the simple countryman. Luxury, oppression and injustice went hand in hand with love of elaborate religious ritual. The combination disgusted him.

Being disgusted by evil is not enough. God told him to tell the people that God too was disgusted, and would judge and punish them with disaster if they didn't repent. It was useless to plead that he wasn't a prophet. God's call made him one. Professional prophets usually pipe to the tune of their paymaster, which is exactly what Amos was later accused of. In fact, he had no choice. His natural indignation, released and inspired by a clear call, exploded into powerful speech. 'The lion has roared; who will not fear? The Lord God has spoken; who can but prophesy?' (Amos 3:8).

Jeroboam had been waging the usual war against Syria, and had succeeded in capturing Damascus. One can imagine the celebration and rejoicing of his people, who would regard victory as a sign of God's approval.

Amos might only be a countryman, but he had the eloquence of Antony addressing the Roman mob after Caesar's death!

First he tells them that God himself would punish Damascus for its sins of merciless cruelty, foreseen by Elisha, and carried out by Hazael (2 Kings 8:11–12; 10:32–33). One can imagine the applause he'd get for that. He then catalogues the crimes of all the other small states that surrounded Israel. Their violent crimes also will receive the punishment due. Applause would mount. Then he turns to Judah. This is coming closer to home. Judah is only accused of failing to keep God's Law. This was precisely the accusation made by Judah against Israel in relation to the calf worship of Bethel. To hear God's judgment pronounced on their self-righteousness and hypocrisy would be doubly welcome.

Then Amos mentions Israel. Tip-toe expectancy. Yes. Israel has been chosen and blessed by God above all other nations (Amos 3:2), and, for that reason, her punishment will be most heavy!

Amos then denounces the evils he has seen, the buying and selling of justice, the prostitution attached to the sanctuary, a practice taken over from Baal worship, the private use of pledges taken for debt, or payment of fines (2:6–8), the tempting of Nazarites, a strictly teetotal religious sect, to break their vows, and the silencing of true prophets (2:11–12). He also attacks the women, whom he likens to cows. It is they who drive their husbands on to oppress the poor, in order to provide the luxuries and expensive wines for which they clamour (4:1–3). He denounces the idle rich, who lounge about, eating, drinking and anointing themselves with perfume, skin lotions and cosmetics. They are like Dives, caring nothing for the poor who lie on their doorsteps (6:1–6). By shutting out all thought of a day of reckoning, they speed its coming with greater violence. How often history has proved this to be true.

Amos also attacked the dishonest traders with their false weights and measures, and adulterated goods, who grumble at the law against sabbath trading (8:4–6).

These were all well-known and accepted evils. The shock came when Amos turned his attack on their worship. It was not against the calves he vented his anger. That was only to be expected from a man of Judah. It was the sabbath hallelujahs coupled with weekday wickedness that caught his fire—'Come to Bethel in order to sin,' he cries with biting sarcasm (4:4–5). 'God hates your festivals, your songs and your sacrifices. He will not listen or accept them.' What God wants is justice for the poor and integrity in their relationship to him (5:21–24).

Then Amos speaks of judgment to come. There has been drought, famine, epidemics, and an invasion of locusts. All these were warnings that should have led them to seek God. Even in military defeats there has been no hint of a national call to prayer (4:6–12). Amos sees all this in a series of visions, and pleads for the people to be spared. But in the vision of the plumbline, Amos realizes that the nation is like a leaning wall. It is out of true. No patching up will save it. The whole structure must be pulled down (7:1–9). Israel, in its present form, has no future. He sees that the Assyrian army will come and destroy both the sanctuaries and the monarchy. The day of the Lord, on which they pinned their hopes, would be a day of destruction not just for their enemies, but for them. It would be a day not of light but of darkness, from which there would be no escape (5:18–20).

Amos makes a passionate plea for repentance so that God would allow at least a remnant to be spared (5:4–15).

This final prophesy leads to an angry response from Amaziah the priest. He sends a messenger to inform the king, and accuses Amos of being in the king of Judah's pay and sent to prophesy disaster on his enemy. This Amos denies. He warns Amaziah of his own approaching fate (7:10–17). He ends with a more terrible warning to those who have rejected his message. There will come a time when they will long to hear a word from God, but he will be silent. This is the most terrible famine of all (Amos 8:11; Deuteronomy 8:3).

The final prophesy recorded is in the form of an astonishing rhetorical question (9:7). The idea that God had been equally active in the history of the Philistines and Syrians was revolutionary. It may well be revolutionary to a lot of Christian thinking today. Israel was no more important in God's eyes than the Ethiopians. To God, British and Bantu are of equal value. Israel was special only because of her calling, and that she had betrayed.

The last five verses were added later. This is clear, for the 'tabernacle of David', the temple, fell only many years later. It provides the Book of Amos with an ending of hope.

Amos was driven out of Bethel. He was lucky to escape with his life!

He, or more likely his disciples, noted down his prophecies, which were later collected and formed into this book. His message remained unheeded until his prophecy was fulfilled. During the exile, it helped to mould the minds of a later generation, the remnant that was to return.

A loving husband   *Hosea*

Unlike Amos, Hosea belonged to Israel, to whom he sometimes refers as Ephraim, or Samaria, the name of its capital city. His message to Israel was born out of his own personal tragedy, his love for an adulterous wife.

Was Hosea led to marry a prostitute as a conscious act of obedience to God? Was he called to allow his private life to become an acted parable to the nation? Some prophets, like Ezekiel, did act out parables, but not with a whole life. Idolatry had always been seen as adultery. The names of Hosea's children speak of God's rejection of the kingdom of Israel. It was a hard burden for the children to bear! Why do parents, for no reason, give their children names that cause them embarrassment and mockery? In this case the children had to share with their father the pain of their family and of the national situation (chapter 1).

Hosea first attacked his nation's idolatry. People believed that only the local Baals could guarantee the fertility of fields and women. The hill shrines provided women for ritual prostitution, just as Hindu temples used to do. But it was their own God, to whom they were wedded by a solemn covenant, who provided for all their needs. People today are seeking success, sexual satisfaction, thrills and relief from boredom in drugs and drink, music and the media. The happiness they seek isn't lasting.

Hosea says that God will call Israel back to himself in a wilderness experience. It was in the desert of Sinai that Israel learned to depend on God for all her essential needs, and found she lacked nothing. Material prosperity had created the discontentment of insatiable appetite, always greedy for more.

The deportation and exile that Amos saw coming as a fearful day of the Lord's anger, Hosea (2:14–23) sees as a second honeymoon! Hosea buys his wife back and, after a time of cleansing separation, restores her as his wife. In such a manner, Israel will be restored (chapter 3).

Israel hadn't broken only the first four commandments, she had broken all ten. When God is disregarded, so are people's rights. After the strong government of Jeroboam II, the evils, which he had controlled, broke out, as Amos foresaw. Note that the evil done by humankind brings evil to the land, sea, and animal kingdom (4:1–3). Hosea attacks priests who profit from people's sin. Punishment largely consisted of fines paid to the shrines. It is a common accusation, even today, that priests batten on people's sins. Certainly charities have benefited from bad consciences (4:6–10).

After attacking lies, murders, drunkenness and idolatry, Hosea goes on to attack adultery. No doubt because of his wife, Hosea blames not the prostitutes, but the men who use them (4:14). This very enlightened viewpoint is far beyond most people's thinking even today.

He then goes on to attack social injustice, the moving of boundary marks, and the annexation of land by the powerful (5:10). Like Amos, he attacks the cheating of the merchants and traders (12:7). Most of all, Hosea attacks the kings, who were nothing but a set of political murderers, as 2 Kings 5 records. 'They consume the men who rule them' (Hosea 7:7). How different was the call and anointing of David (Hosea 8:4). Not only do these kings act like bandits, they create the chaos in which bandits can terrorize the common people. It is a situation similar to that of China before the Communists took over. Hosea also attacks their reliance on foreign powers (2 Kings 15:19–20; 17:3–5), allying alternatively with Egypt and Assyria (Hosea 5:13; 7:11). He compares them to a silly dove, cooing love songs in every direction, and to a prostitute renting lovers (8:9). He also blazes with anger at the calf installed by Jeroboam I. It was an insult to God, a flagrant breaking of the second commandment for purely political purposes (8:5).

The first response to Hosea's message seems to have been a show of repentance (Hosea 6). The motive was fear. The means was to double the sacrifices, which God didn't accept anyway. The result was short-lived. No change took place in their lifestyle. They had only been offering God the kind of protection money they had sent to Egypt and Assyria. When God didn't deliver they stopped. How many people today give up on God because, after a few prayers, he doesn't give them success in an exam or business venture?

Hosea's teaching is summed up in the key verse 6:6. The Hebrew word *hesed* translated as 'mercy' in the AV is, in the RSV, translated as 'steadfast love'. It implies a relationship of love and loyalty. This, as Hosea had so painfully experienced, was costly. It was the kind of love God had given Israel. It was the kind of love he looked for in return.

Knowledge of God is not mere head knowledge, not just knowledge about God, as in Hosea 8:2. The word refers to a deep intimacy, experienced as a result of mutual self-giving. In Scripture it is the usual word for the marital act of love (Genesis 4:1). Amos had taught that what God wanted was for justice—right dealing—'to roll down like water'. Social and economic justice is an aspect of love. Too often, however, it has been generated by hatred. The result is then, only too often, injustice in a different form. What God wants, says Hosea, is a loving relationship with us. Sacrifices, gifts, religious services, all these can be cheap substitutes. It is us that God wants. From such a relationship of love and loyalty a life of obedience will flow (John 14:15–24).

Hosea's message is not heeded. The penitential tears soon dry.

Hosea now clearly warns Israel that the state will be destroyed, and they will go into exile, back into slavery. He mentions both Egypt and Assyria. Maybe his reference to Egypt was more symbolic. Amos had seen clearly that the threat was coming from the north, not the south. The reaction to this prophesy was to call him mad (Hosea 9:7). In chapter 10 his reference to Assyria is specific (Hosea 10:6). He pleads for true repentance (Hosea 10:12). 'Sow ... righteousness, reap in mercy; break up your fallow ground.'

In chapter 11 the tone changes. Anger is the other side of the coin of love. The opposite of love is not anger but indifference. God is now pictured as a father, tenderly teaching his child to walk. All through their history he has drawn Israel to himself with love. He will, when necessary, chastise, but he can never abandon his child. So there is hope. We don't learn to understand God's Fatherhood by looking at a human father, however good. We learn to understand fatherhood by coming to know God. We learn about his Fatherhood most fully in his relationship with Jesus.

Breaking fallow ground is hard work. Learning to pray from the heart and changing one's lifestyle is not easy. Hosea refers to Jacob's long night of struggle with God's angel at Penuel (Genesis 32:24–31). He had power and prevailed. If the people of Israel want such prevailing power with God they must wait patiently for him in prayer, and be prepared to pay the cost, as Jacob did (Hosea 12:3–6). God cries, 'O Israel, you have destroyed yourself' (13:9). But God has power over the grave. Beyond the cross lies resurrection (13:14). It is a wonderful foretaste of the gospel. It is quoted by St Paul in 1 Corinthians 15:55 and read at funeral services.

Hosea ends with a final plea (chapter 14), full of promise and hope. Verse 8 climaxes in a dialogue of love between Ephraim and God. Verse 9 is an anticlimax. It is not by Hosea, but the comment of a scribe.

Hosea has been called the prophet of love. There is another possible interpretation of his experience. Did he really marry Gomer out of conscious obedience, knowing her to be a prostitute? Did he then learn to love and forgive her because he knew that God loved and would forgive Israel? Or was it the other way round? Maybe Hosea married Gomer because he loved her, and only slowly realized her infidelity, and the probability that his second and third children were not his own. It was she who left him, going possibly from lover to lover, until her value was so low that Hosea was able to buy her back. What an agony of heartbreak. What terrible humiliation! He would have no assurance that she would not leave him again. Her penitence had never lasted long. His action would certainly be condemned by his neighbours. Even today, how many would understand? So great was his love. He must have been shown, perhaps in a flash of revelation, that this was how God felt about Israel. It would have transformed his message. So, a book that starts with harsh condemnation ends with the pleading of love. Hosea could then look back on the pain of his marriage and see that there was a purpose in it all. God had been in it from the start. In the same way we can look back on painful experiences that have brought us more deeply into the loving heart of God, and say with gratitude, 'It was his will for us.'

For further reading

Psalms 15; 26; 50; 51; James 2:1–17; 5:1–9

For group discussion

1. Are the evils denounced by Amos with us today? Are there new ones?

2. How does your church link worship to social action?

3. Why are revivals so often short-lived in their effects?

For private reflection

1. What does a wilderness experience mean to you? How can it become a second honeymoon?

2. Is there any painful experience you can now look back on with gratitude?

3. How can we grow in our experience of God?

10

Three Prophets of Judah

Isaiah 1–39; Micah; Nahum

While Amos and Hosea were prophesying to Israel, God was raising up prophets to speak to Judah. The greatest of these was Isaiah, whose prophecies take up the first thirty-nine chapters of the book called by his name.

A counsellor at court   Isaiah 1–39

Isaiah grew up at the court of Azariah, or Uzziah as he was called. Uzziah was one of the best kings Judah had known and he reigned for fifty-two years (2 Kings 14:21–22; 15:1–7). For the last few years of his life he suffered from leprosy. According to the Chronicler, writing long after the event, this was a punishment for presumption, performing a ritual reserved to priests (2 Chronicles 26:16–21). He had to live apart and let his son Jotham rule for him. It was a tragic end for a great and good man. When he died, Isaiah must have felt shattered.

He went into the temple to pray, and there he had a vision of the glory of God (Isaiah 6). It filled him with awe and a sense of sin, both that of his people and his own. Amos and Hosea had no such sense of personal sin. Isaiah's tongue was the source of his trouble. Both prophets, priests and courtiers were notorious for their easy speeches and lies. All political figures are under pressure to twist, or at least, to use modern parliamentary jargon, to be economical with the truth. Cleansed by a burning coal, taken from the altar, Isaiah hears God's challenge. 'Who will go for us?' He responds by self-surrender. 'Here am I. Send me.'

The call of God comes to people in different ways. It may be a direct appointment by God, in a vision, as with Moses and St Paul. It may come through a leader with spiritual authority, as with Saul, David and Elisha. Or it may come by a realization of some great need, and a strong inner urge to respond, as with Mother Teresa today.

The commission Isaiah was given must have sounded harsh. He was to warn his people of coming disaster. He was told that they would close their ears, but he was to carry on until the disaster fell.

Why should God call anyone to a mission that is bound to fail? For a very good reason. His words, and those of Amos and Hosea, would be remembered after the calamity had fallen. The captive Jews would realize they had been warned, and had brought the destruction on themselves. This conviction would bring them back to God.

In those early days Isaiah's message resembled that of Amos. It is summed up in the passionate outpouring of 1:1–20. His detailed denunciations are found in 3:12–26. Verse 12 probably refers to Athaliah, who seized power after Jehu's slaughter (2 Kings 11:1–3). Isaiah's description of the finery of ladies at court is particularly vivid.

His beautiful 'Song of the Vineyard', referring to God as his beloved, pictures Judah as fruitless. The wild grapes of wrath are catalogued in a series of woes against social and economic injustice, careless luxury, pride, mockery, deliberate self-deception, drunkenness and corruption. They are all very familiar in our society today. Jesus used the imagery of this parable in a parable of his own. It was well understood, and the anger it provoked helped to bring about his death (Luke 20:9–19).

During his ministry, Isaiah was led to counsel two kings in times of national crisis.

The first king was Ahaz, and the crisis was a combined attack on Judah by Israel and Syria (2 Kings 16; Isaiah 7:1–2). Ahaz' reaction was to turn to Assyria for help. Assyria was the rising imperial power that was threatening all the small states. It was a case of calling in the wolf to drive out the foxes.

Isaiah had many things to say. First he tells Ahaz not to be afraid. The power of Israel and Syria is only the power of men, Pekah and Rezin, and both will soon be broken. In fact Pekah was murdered by Hoshea (2 Kings 15:30—the action here is said to be in Jotham's reign. Isaiah is more likely to be correct).

Isaiah then offered to give Ahaz a sign to confirm this prophecy. Ahaz piously rejected this as tempting God (compare Deuteronomy 6:16; Matthew 4:7). We have seen, in the story of Gideon, the difference between an unbelieving demand for God to prove himself, which is what Ahaz claims to reject, and the request, in faith, for a sign to confirm God's leading. This is what Isaiah was offering. However, Ahaz's real reason for refusing a sign was that he didn't want to know. He didn't want to know because he didn't want to obey, a very good reason for the refusal of many to listen to the claims of the gospel.

Isaiah offers Ahaz a sign nonetheless. He foretells the imminent birth of a child to be called Immanuel, meaning 'God with us'. Before the child is weaned, both kings will be dead.

The Hebrew word translated 'virgin' in the AV doesn't have the technical meaning we give it. It simply implies a young woman. But the

102

virgin birth, recorded by St Luke as well as St Matthew, does not depend for its truth on the quotation of this text. A child was born as a sign to Ahaz that God was with his people, and an alliance with Assyria was foolish and unnecessary. But the child's birth and name was a foreshadowing of Christ, our true Immanuel. Men and women, guided by the spirit of God, speak of truths deeper than their understanding. Another example of this is Caiaphas speaking of Jesus' death (John 11:49–52).

Isaiah already had a son, who went with him to visit Ahaz. This son's name meant 'A remnant will return'. Isaiah's vision had shown him that Judah would be destroyed, but that a faithful few would return to rebuild, and this was an important part of his message.

Isaiah then went and begot another son—not Immanuel—whose name meant Speed (Isaiah 8:3). This was another confirmation that the fall of the two kings would be speedy. It was. As we have seen, Pekah was murdered by Hoshea. The Assyrian wolf finished off both states in two bites. Tiglath Pilesar III, referred to as Pul, had been nibbling away at them for some time (2 Kings 15:19–20), and was only too delighted to respond to Ahaz's invitation. Then, in 732BC, Damascus fell, and Syria lost its independence. Ten years later, in 722BC, Shalmaneser took Samaria, and deported its population, scattering them throughout the empire (2 Kings 18:9–12). In our day the former USSR used this policy extensively, especially in the Baltic states.

Finally, Isaiah warned Ahaz that Assyria would come up against Judah too. It would be useless to seek an alliance with Egypt, which was a broken reed. Worse than useless was turning for help from mediums, as Saul had done! 'Should not a people seek their God?' God is a sanctuary to those who trust him. To others he is a stone of stumbling, and a snare (compare 1 Peter 2:6–8).

Ahaz did not heed Isaiah's advice. It was useless to say more. Isaiah had his prophecies written down. They were sealed up in a book, and in the hearts of his disciples. They and his family, signs of God in the midst of the land, and a foretaste of a faithful remnant, settled down to seek and wait upon God (Isaiah 8:16–18). The Church is called sometimes to speak, sometimes to act. Sometimes it is called to silence, to delve more deeply into God, watching, waiting, fasting and interceding. It is out of such silence that new vision and new opportunities are born.

Years passed, and the mighty armies of the most ruthlessly efficient war machine the world had ever seen rolled over the surrounding lands, including the outlying territory of Judah. Isaiah describes the appalling scenes in his prophecies of woes, or burdens (chapters 13–14). There is no need to read all this, but it is important to note Isaiah's attitude. First, he is moved to tears by the anguish of Judah's traditional enemies (Isaiah 16:9; 21:3–6; 22:4). There is no gloating or triumphalism, only compassion. Secondly, he sees Assyria as a rod in the hands of a heavenly Father, chastising his son. The king of Assyria, planning to achieve his own ambitious purposes, is in fact serving God. When God's purposes are achieved, then he will be cast aside and punished for his crimes and for his pride. Assyria will be humbled, Judah restored. When disaster overtakes the world, we can hold hard to Isaiah's faith that God is still in control (Isaiah 10:5–27).

Those who seek the Lord are rewarded with new insights. Isaiah's vision of the child Immanuel gets stronger and clearer. In some mysterious way, he is to be God himself, Father, King and Prince of Peace, bringing in a kingdom of peace and justice for all peoples and all time (Isaiah 9:6–7). Humanly speaking he will be a son of David, wiser and more righteous than Solomon (Isaiah 11:1–8). In his kingdom the harmony between men and women and the animal kingdom, broken by the fall, will be restored. Darwin noted that animals with no previous knowledge of humans show no fear of them, and the story of St Francis taming the wolf echoes the prophecies of Isaiah.

As the political scene got more dangerous and desperate, Isaiah's vision of the kingdom becomes more glorious and real. Even in the midst of suffering and death, Isaiah calls on the people of Jerusalem to join him in rejoicing and praising God. We can join in his rejoicing as we meditate upon the golden verses of his prophecies (Isaiah 12; 24:13–15; 25:1, 6–9; 26:1–4, 8–9, 12–13, 20; 32:1–8, 13–20; 30:15–18, 20–21, 29).

Isaiah's vision of the future included hope for nations other than his own. He foresaw a time when God would be worshipped both in Egypt and Assyria. Together with Judah they would be linked by a highway of holiness (Isaiah 19:19–25; 35:1–10). There is indeed such a highway linking Christians of every nation, holding them together in prayer, even when their countries are divided by war. Christ's Spirit can lift us above the passionate nationalistic feelings and viewpoints fed by propaganda, into love, and into sharing in the viewpoint of God. For such Christians peace is not distant, or round the corner, but here and now.

Ahaz died, and his son Hezekiah came to the throne. He was a good king, faithful to God. It is interesting that included amongst the idols he destroyed was the brazen serpent Moses had made to stop a plague of such creatures. It had become an object of worship (2 Kings 18:1–8).

There is always a danger that symbols such as crosses, statues and icons, given to draw us closer to God, can become treasured and revered in themselves in a manner bordering on idolatry. Fear of this has led, at various times, to their violent destruction, signs of which we can still see in many churches and cathedrals today. Greater centrality and deeper devotion given to Christ himself restores these things to their proper place.

Hezekiah broke with his father's policy of trying to appease Assyria and, when Shalmaneser had finished with Israel, he turned his attention to attacking a number of Judah's fortified cities.

Hezekiah's first thought was to turn to Egypt for help. Isaiah vigorously opposed this policy (Isaiah 30:1–7; 31:1–3). His message was the same as that given to Ahaz. Judah must return to God (30:15–18). God would guide them safely (30:20–21). Then great would be the rejoicing, for God himself would overthrow the Assyrian army (30:29–31; 31:5 8–9).

Easy for a prophet to prophesy, but how can a ruler take such a risk? So might we think. Actually, Egypt was in such a state of internal strife, she would have been useless as an ally. She was then only a 'has-been' empire, living on a shaky reputation. To live by faith is practical. However, Hezekiah first tried the familiar tactics of buying off Assyria. This only delayed the final attack on Jerusalem.

The dramatic story of what followed is recorded in 2 Kings 18 and 19 which is inserted wholesale into the Book of Isaiah as chapters 36 and 37. The Assyrian commander calls on the Jews to surrender. The gods of other cities have not been able to save, so neither will their god. So he proclaimed. Hezekiah goes into the temple to pray, and sends for Isaiah, who prophesies that God will disperse the Assyrian army by sending a rumour of trouble at home. That actually happened, but it only provided a respite. Rabshakeh writes to Hezekiah repeating his contemptuous challenge, and saying he will return to the attack.

Again Hezekiah turns to God, pleading with him to defend Jerusalem, that all may know that he alone is God of all the earth. The words recall Elijah's prayer on Mount Carmel. Isaiah repeats his assurance that Assyria will not be able to take the city. The army, now led by King Sennacherib himself, besieges the city. Then the miracle happens. The biblical writer speaks of an angel of the Lord smiting the camp. The Greek historian Herodotus wrote that a swarm of rats invaded the camp and chewed their bow strings. The two accounts could both be true, as rats might have led to an outbreak of plague. If so, Sennacherib may have struck camp to avoid death by disease. He went home to meet death at the hand of his own sons. The date was 681BC.

Those who do not believe in miracles will always try and explain them away. To those who look at world affairs with the eyes of faith, God still works miracles. Maybe the collapse of the Berlin Wall was one of them, and the astonishing opening up of Albania and Nepal to the gospel, after years of faithful prayer.

Hezekiah too came face to face with death (2 Kings 20; Isaiah 38). Isaiah was told to tell him to prepare for death by setting his house in order. Hezekiah wept and prayed, and God responded by sending Isaiah to him again to promise him another fifteen years of life. No one can explain the sign of the sundial. Unlike the story of the sun standing still, it is not a quotation from poetry. It is, however, an illustration of the time clock of Hezekiah's life being put back. Isaiah was also led to apply a remedy for his sickness. Infection can cause general septicaemia which a poultice can draw to a head. The relationship between medical science and prayer and faith is mysterious, but it is experienced, and is an increasingly recognized fact.

Hezekiah's prayer of thanksgiving (Isaiah 38:9–19) is deeply moving. Very significant is his comment, 'By these things men live.' Over and over again we see how it is in such experiences of crisis, pain, fear and closeness to death, that the human spirit can grow.

This experience did not give Hezekiah political wisdom. When the king of Babylon sent him presents and letters of sympathy, Hezekiah failed to recognize this as the political manoeuvre of an up-and-coming world power. Moved no doubt by vanity, he showed off all his treasures. Isaiah rebuked him for his short-sighted foolishness. He prophesied that Babylon would one day do to Judah what Assyria had done to Israel. Hezekiah's reaction was only relief that peace would last his time (chapter 39; compare Matthew 16:1–3). *Après moi, le déluge.*

There is a tradition that Isaiah was put to death by Hezekiah's notoriously evil son Manasseh who had him sawn in half. Hebrews 11:34–38 refers to this. Isaiah was one of that noble band of faith of whom 'the world was not worthy'. He died in faith 'not having received the promises, but having seen them from afar' (Hebrews 11:13; Isaiah 2:2–4; 29:18–19; 32:1–4).

A prophet in the provinces   *Micah*

Micah lived at the same time as Isaiah and may have known him, or even have been one of his disciples. He came from Moresheth in the southern foothills, one of the twelve provincial cities overrun by the Assyrians before they besieged Jerusalem.

He started to prophesy before the fall of Samaria, and ended by prophesying the fall of Jerusalem. Luckily for him, Hezekiah was a king who respected prophets, so Micah was not put to death as a traitor. This fact was quoted about seventy years later, to save Jeremiah from being killed after making the same prophesy (Jeremiah 26:11–19). Micah's message was much the same as that of Isaiah and the other prophets of that time. If God has something important to say to us he often bombards us with it from all directions! The text of Micah's book is confusing. The AV brings out the richness and depth of some passages with matchless beauty, but it is advisable also to read and compare it with modern translations based on more ancient and reliable Hebrew texts. Prophecies of different periods are mixed up and some, such as 7:8–20, are not by Micah at all.

Micah sees God coming as a consuming and refining fire. Samaria will be destroyed because of her idols. Her foundations will be laid bare. They were indeed, and one can see some of them today. But more than stone foundations are referred to here. War, famine, loss of employment and possessions, disease and death, all these things shake us to our foundations. Then we discover whether or not we have anything left to stand on (compare Matthew 7:24–27). It is a terrifying and life-changing experience, but many have later thanked God for it.

Micah howls with pain as he sees the advancing Assyrian army destroy, one by one, the twelve provincial towns, including his own. Each lament is a pun on their names—for example, Maroth means bitterness. The greedy landowners, who have seized the lands of their poorer neighbours, will now see their own land measured off and taken by others. No year of Jubilee will return it.

Like the other prophets, Micah meets ridicule, and is told to shut up. God is not responsible for these evils, he is told. God only does good to his people, who 'walk uprightly'. Micah reacts to this nauseating protestation of innocence by making more detailed accusations. The vivid imagery he uses (3:2–3) is like that of the French peasant before the French Revolution who said of the noble landlords, 'They crop us as sheep crop grass.' Micah then turns from the nobles to the prophets who seek to please their paymaster by crying, 'Peace, peace.' Russian Orthodox bishops, appointed by an atheist committee as men who would be subservient, were allowed to attend meetings of the World Council of Churches. There they mouthed bland statements declaring that Christians in Russia had freedom, and all was well with the Church. With the advent of glasnost, the truth, long suspected, came out into the open. Russia's true prophets, released from prison and labour camps, now openly proclaim their message of faith which they previously had to circulate secretly. Like them, Micah is a true prophet, filled with the Spirit, and unafraid to speak words of judgment.

If Micah howls with pain, he does not howl without hope. Micah 4:2–4 is lifted straight out of Isaiah 2:2–5. There were no laws of copyright in those days. It would be fairer to say that the origin of these verses in Micah and Isaiah is uncertain. Also any prophecy made by a prophet could be given a final editing by a later follower.

Micah also shares Isaiah's belief in a faithful remnant that would return. It is also to be found in the Book of Deuteronomy where it may have originated (Deuteronomy 30:3). The verses of 4:8–13 belong, however, to a much later period, that of Jeremiah, when the advancing

107

army was that of Babylon. They contain a wonderful vision of the exile seen as the birthpangs of a purified nation—and end with a wider vision that foreshadows the worldwide Church.

In chapter 5, Micah picks up Isaiah's developing prophecy about Immanuel. Micah sees him as a king, a descendent of David, to be born in David's city. How breathtakingly wonderful that his prophesy should be brought to fulfilment hundreds of years later, by a Roman emperor deciding to impose a poll tax! In that day, God's people will no longer depend on other people but on God (5:7). Note the repetition of God's words 'I will'.

It brings us back to Micah's first prophecy, that behind all the terrible political events of his day God is at work. In chapter 6 Micah pictures God as summoning mountains and earth as witnesses to his case against his people. What case can they bring against him who has done nothing but good? His only reward is the slaughter of thousands of rams. Note how these prophets protest against concentration on animal sacrifice. One wonders what the Jewish state of Israel would do today if they regained control of the temple area. Would the right-wing religious party manage to get the temple rebuilt, and, if so, could they restore the sacrificial system in this day and age? It may be just as well for them that the Dome of the Rock makes this impossible!

Micah sums up what God desires from us in the lovely simplicity of verse 8. 'This is what Yahweh asks of you: only this, to act justly, to love tenderly, and to walk humbly with your God' (JB). Justice, tender love and humility, in an ongoing relationship with God, these are qualities, now as then, conspicuous by their absence. 'Give the least. Get the most,' expressed their lifestyle, and ours. We might add, 'Work less for more pay' and, 'Demand highest value for lowest price.' The result is a heart that is never satisfied. Idols of power, money and sensual enjoyment bring no lasting joy. In the hour of need they cannot save. In chapter 7 we see Micah's despair. Good and honest men no longer exist. Not even members of one's own family can be trusted. Hosea knew this. So did Jeremiah. Did Micah also share this experience?

Again, like Isaiah, Micah decides that all he can do now is to wait upon God. God is his saviour. People may block their ears, but God will hear.

This is Micah's final word. The last verses contain a prophecy that belongs to the exiles in Babylon. It is a beautiful picture of the people accepting their suffering in patience and hope. It leads to an outpouring of praise and trust in the limitless forgiveness and mercy of God, ending the book with fulfilment and hope.

Nahum and the sack of Nineveh (612BC)   *Nahum*

Assyria was the most ruthlessly cruel of all the empires. The horror felt in Europe at the expansion of Nazi Germany is as nothing to the horror felt by the Middle Eastern states as the Assyrian war machine rolled over them.

When the armies of Babylon sacked Nineveh in 612BC, forcing the Assyrians to suffer the fate they had inflicted on all their neighbours, a cry of jubilation went up. Nahum describes the assault on the city, and shared in the jubilation.

His book starts with an acrostic poem on God's anger against Nineveh. Each verse starts with consecutive letters of the Hebrew alphabet.

Then follows a series of short prophecies to Judah and Assyria: verses 9–10 to Judah, verse 11 to Assyria (the wicked plotter may have been Sennacherib), verses 12–13 to Judah, verse 14 to the king of Nineveh, verse 15 to Judah.

Chapter 2 is a dramatic description of the assault. The lion was a symbol of Assyria. In chapter 3 Nineveh is warned to learn from the fall of Thebes (called 'No' in the AV) that her defences are useless.

With the fall of Nineveh, the Assyrian Empire collapsed, and that of Babylon took its place.

Nahum lacked the wide vision of Isaiah, but two golden verses can be culled from this book: Nahum 1:7, and 1:15—which has inspired many Christian songs. For these we owe him a debt of gratitude.

For further reading

Psalms 46; 57; 61; 91; 124

For group discussion

1. What evils can the tongue commit? How can we control it?

2. In witnessing to the gospel, how would you distinguish between the time to keep silent and the time to speak?

3. How do you think God is at work in the political scene today?

For private reflection

1. What awakens our sense of sinfulness?

2. 'Here am I. Send me.' Is there anything to which God is calling you to make this response?

3. If the foundations of your life were shaken, what do you think would remain?

11

The Advent of Disaster

2 Kings 21–25; Zephaniah; Deuteronomy 4–11; 30; Jeremiah; Obadiah; Habakkuk

Background to the prophecies   2 Kings 21–25

Disaster overtakes a nation when all efforts at reform have failed. Reform for the kingdom of Judah had to start with a return to God, with worship, and the honouring of his name. The fate of the northern kingdom of Israel was a fearful warning.

Hezekiah's reign had seen the first effort at reform. The temple, which had fallen into disrepair, was cleaned up. Its treasury, depleted by Ahab, was replenished, and the king called his people to a celebration of the Passover in a manner not seen since the days of Solomon (2 Chronicles 29–30). Those who took part in this joyful experience returned home and smashed the altars in the groves, and on the high places which, for centuries, had been tolerated (2 Chronicles 31:1). God had honoured the reform and the faith of their king, and Jerusalem had been saved from the army of Assyria. Then Hezekiah was succeeded by Manasseh, the most evil king ever to sit on the throne of David.

Why is it that, so often, sons react violently against the ways of a godly father? Is it that some forms of godliness are rigid and censorious, lacking in love and laughter, and time given to the family? With Absalom it was overindulgence, and lack of discipline that led to disaster. Manasseh was only twelve when he succeeded to the throne, so, perhaps his almost passionate idolatry was taught him by reactionary advisers, trying to put the clock back on reform.

When Manasseh grew up, he not only restored idolatry, even to the temple, but introduced witchcraft and human sacrifice. He even sacrificed one of his own sons to the fiery throat of Molech (2 Kings 21:1–6).

Manasseh reigned fifty years, so these evils took a strong hold. According to the Chronicler (2 Chronicles 33:1–20), Manasseh later repented, after being deported by the Assyrians, and, after his release, tried to undo his evil work. Outside sources affirm that he was, throughout his reign, a vassal of Assyria. Even if the story of his repentance is true, his reform was ineffective and was reversed by his son Ammon.

Ammon's reign was mercifully short. After two years his own servants murdered him. The priestly party was restored to power, and Ammon's son Josiah, a boy of eight, was brought up to be a devout worshipper of the God of Israel. As Josiah was growing up, the thunder of another prophet rang in his ears—that of Zephaniah.

Zephaniah

Zephaniah warned that God would punish idolaters and all those who profited from wickedness. He would search out the complacent and the scoffers. Judgment would fall and their riches would not save them (chapter 1). He called for a return to God in a spirit of meekness, a spirit willing to be disciplined and guided. Like Isaiah, he sees both judgment and hope for all the nations, not just Jerusalem—that 'rejoicing and careless city' (chapter 2). He, too, foresees the survival of a faithful remnant.

His book is like a dark cave, but the darkness is the setting for one of the brightest jewels in the Old Testament. So read and search it out.

Josiah and the Book of Deuteronomy   *2 Kings 22–23*

When Josiah was twenty-six he decided to repair and clean up the temple again. While this was being done, a book was discovered. It was probably the Book of Deuteronomy. When it was read to him, the king was horrified to learn how far his people had fallen away from God's Law.

The 'Second Law'   Deuteronomy 4–11; 30

We have already looked at extracts from this book when studying the life of Moses and the Law. Now chapters 4–11 and chapter 30 need further study.

In chapter 4 the people are warned that if, after entering Canaan, they start to worship other gods, they will be scattered among the nations, (4:26–27). But note the promise of return if then they repent (4:29).

In chapter 5 the Ten Commandments are restated. *Deutero Nomos* means Second Law, and chapter 6 starts with the summary quoted by Jesus as the first great commandment. The importance of parents teaching it to their children is stressed. Religion starts in the home. How much of the present decline started when indifferent parents left the job to Sunday Schools?

Chapter 7 commands that no treaty be made with the Canaanite people, nor any intermarriage. Disobedience in this matter was one of the main causes of idolatry. The Israelites were reminded that God had called them, not because they were strong, but because they were weak, and because God was faithful and merciful. He was their strength, and, through his commandments, called them to be holy as he is holy.

Chapter 8 calls them to remember all God had done for them. This thankful remembering of the past is very important in the Old Testament, and the Psalms are full of it. For us too, remembering what God has done for us is a source of strength for the present, and hope for the future. Verse 3 provided a source of strength to Jesus when tempted in the wilderness. Verses 11–17 warn of the danger, in days of prosperity, of giving the credit to oneself and forgetting God.

Over and over again, chapter 9 speaks of a stiff-necked and rebellious people. What God wants for them is set forth in chapter 10:12–13 in words that recall those of Micah (6:8). In chapter 11 and again in chapter 30, Moses sets before his people a blessing and a curse. In chapter 28 he prophesies they will disobey and reap the curse, but in chapter 30 he prophesies that after that they will obey and reap the blessing.

This teaching had been given by Amos, Hosea and Isaiah. They had been disregarded, but this book, claiming to have the authority of Moses himself, made a deep impression on the king. He summoned all the leading men of Judah, and himself read the book to them, and led them in renewing their covenant with God.

The Book of Chronicles describes how Josiah set about undoing the work of Manasseh and Ammon, throwing down altars, destroying idols and expelling those practising sodomy and witchcraft. Finally, he celebrated another great Passover. If Hezekiah's was deemed to be the greatest since Solomon, this was the greatest since the days of Samuel (2 Chronicles 35:18; compare 2 Chronicles 30:21–26).

Never since David had there been a king so utterly devoted to God. Yet, within a few years, he was killed by the Egyptians, in the battle of Megiddo.

The Chronicler makes it clear that Egypt was marching through Judah only in order to attack Assyria. There was no wish to fight Josiah, and a message was sent to tell him so. But, like the Belgian king of World War I, Josiah bravely refused to give passage. The Chronicler believed the message was a divine warning which Josiah failed to recognize (2 Chronicles 35:20–24). Was this a priestly effort to justify God? When good men come to a sticky end it poses a problem. Years later, the Book of Job showed that it is wiser to pour out one's true feelings, to argue and fight with God, than try to find arguments to justify him!

It was a tragic end to a good king and to the last hope of reform. After this the end was swift. It is set out in 2 Kings 23:31—25:30. The prophet who dominated these years of final disaster was Jeremiah.

The Book of Jeremiah

Jeremiah is one of the greatest of all the prophets. He is certainly the most human, for we know more about him than any of the others. Not only the facts about his life, but his feelings and fears, the secrets of his inner life are revealed in moving and passionate language. His imagery is so beautifully expressed that his book is a bit like *Hamlet*—full of quotations. It is not arranged in chronological order, and to read it straight through is to lose oneself in a chaotic jumble. So we'll have to hop forward and back to make any sense of it.

His call and early years

Jeremiah's call is described in Jeremiah 1:1–10, 17–19. He did not want to be a prophet. Like Moses he made excuses. He pleaded his youth, but his plea was not accepted. Adult wisdom was not required. Jeremiah was to be a mouthpiece for God. What was required was open eyes and open ears, combined with courage and obedience. Like Isaiah, he would be given a message of judgment for everyone from the king downward, but God would defend him against them all.

The period before Josiah's reforms are covered in 2:1—3:5, 19–25, and chapter 10. Jeremiah attacks the idolatry introduced by Manasseh. He uses Hosea's imagery of the unfaithful wife, and Isaiah's imagery of the vine. Both were traditional pictures of Israel. With amazingly patient humility, he sees God pleading with his people. No other nation has deserted their God. Perhaps, we may think, because no other god makes such ethical demands! Jeremiah puts it differently. They prefer stagnant water, drawn from cracked cisterns of their own making, to the pure fresh water of God's spring (compare John 4:10–14). Experience will teach them the consequence of their choice (Jeremiah 2:19). During the time of reform, Jeremiah threw his youthful energy into promoting Josiah's reforms and the renewal of the covenant (11:1—12:6).

This involved attacking the hill shrines, including the one at Anathoth where his own father was priest.

Jeremiah's family turned against him. He had to leave home and flee for his life. He left with a mind full of questions, and a heart full of bitterness (12:1–3). Instead of sympathy, God gave him a rebuke for his faintheartedness. There would be worse to come. Sympathy can weaken. The word comfort means to strengthen. When Jesus offered the Holy Spirit as comforter, he was not offering us a cushion, let alone a Linus blanket!

Prophecies during the reign of Jehoiakim

Leaving Anathoth, Jeremiah came to Jerusalem. There, in the holy city, site of the temple, the centre of Josiah's reforms, he would have expected to find true devotion to God.

His idealism must have been shattered by what he discovered. The reform had been superficial. A pious façade concealed a society stinking with corruption. As Jeremiah explored the city, he found all the sins denounced by earlier prophets: sexual immorality (5:7–9); corrupt prophets and priests (5:13–14; 6:14; 8:11); social injustice (5:25–29); greed (6:13) together with meaningless sacrifices (6:20). Even idolatry continued secretly in private homes (7:17–18). Despite Josiah's renewal of the covenant, the ordinary people had not returned to God (6:16–19; 8:4–7).

At first, Jeremiah thought of appealing to the leaders. Here too, he was disillusioned (5:1–5). They did not believe in a truly living God. God was a name to be sworn by, someone to be found in a book they didn't want to read, being too full of things they didn't want to hear (6:10).

At the time of his call Jeremiah had been shown a vision of an almond tree, and a pot that was boiling over from a northern direction. The almond, as the first tree to blossom, was called the 'wakeful tree'. These visions woke Jeremiah to see a new danger gathering against Judah. The power of Assyria had been crushed, but now Babylon was in the ascendant.

After Megiddo, Jehoiakim had been installed as king by Pharaoh Neco in place of his brother, and had been subjected to Egyptian control. Four years later, at the battle of Carchemish, 605BC, Egypt was defeated by the army of Nebuchadnezzar (Jeremiah 46:1–2). Jeremiah was convinced that God would use the Babylonians to execute his judgment on Judah just as he had used Assyria to execute it upon Israel. The question was, if King Josiah's effort to reform had failed, could the preaching of a prophet succeed? Was it now too late? Jeremiah 8:20 (together with Luke 19:42) is one of the saddest verses in the Bible. Like Jesus, who foresaw the destruction of both temple and city by the Romans, Jeremiah weeps for his city (compare Matthew 23:34–39).

Unlike Jesus, or perhaps not so very unlike, all Jeremiah wanted to do was to run away (9:1–2). Instead God told him to go and stand at the temple gates, and to say all that God gave him, no matter what the consequences. And he obeyed.

Jeremiah's temple sermon is found in chapters 7 and 26. Shiloh, the place where the ark was first kept, had been destroyed (1 Samuel 4:3–11). Jeremiah's audience believed they were safe from all attack, because God would never allow his temple to suffer damage. Hadn't the experience of Sennacherib's army proved this? But their security was a delusion. The two situations were different. Then there was faith, now, only presumption. Jeremiah denounced this presumption with the terrible judgment, later quoted by Jesus in a similar situation (Jeremiah 7:11; Mark 11:17). He was nearly lynched for his pains.

Jeremiah's prophecy of the city's destruction was confirmed when God sent him to visit a potter (18:1–6). Like clay in a potter's hand, the city was marred by its intractable disobedience. It had to be crushed in order to be remade. Here again, one of the main themes of the Bible is repeated. It is prayerfully expressed in the familiar chorus:

Spirit of the Living God fall afresh on me.
Melt me, mould me, fill me, use me.

Jeremiah then visited the Valley of Hinnom where, during the reign of Manasseh, human sacrifice had taken place. There, in a passion of anger, he smashed a pot as an acted parable of the city's destruction (chapter 19). For this further provocation, Pashur, the governor of the temple, had him arrested and put in the stocks (chapter 20).

It may have been at this time (the chronology is not clear) that Jeremiah got his disciple, Baruch, to write down his prophecies in a scroll. He then told him to read it by the temple. Bravely, Baruch did this (chapter 36). The scroll was seized and read to the king. Jehoiakim cut it in pieces and burnt it, ordering both Jeremiah and Baruch to be arrested. Friends, however, kept them hidden. Jeremiah then dictated a second scroll, adding further prophecies relating to the king himself (36:29–32; 22:13–19). This prophecy wasn't quite fulfilled, so perhaps Jeremiah's anger got mixed up in it. But Jehoiakim's son only reigned a hundred days before being taken as a captive into Babylon.

Maybe Baruch hoped that he would somehow reap a reward for all he had suffered on God's behalf. Perhaps, when disaster overtook the city, he would be protected and receive favourable treatment. Together with Jeremiah, he was in fact offered this by the Babylonian commander after the city fell. Jeremiah warns him to expect nothing but his life (chapter 45).

There are some Christians who believe that faithfulness to God will exempt them from sharing in the suffering of the world. It did not exempt Jesus. Far from it. He chose, for the sake of love, to identify himself with the pain of the world. Faithfulness to him means sharing his cross. If, in any instance, there is a special deliverance, it is because God is fulfilling his purpose, not giving us reward. God has no favourites.

Some have thought that the original model for the suffering servant, described in Isaiah 53, was Jeremiah. Certainly he was 'a man of sorrows and acquainted with grief'. Scattered throughout his book are a collection of his spiritual outpourings. These make very moving reading, and find echoes in the Book of Job. They are to be found in 15:10–11, 15–21; 17:9–10, 14–18; 18:18–23 and 20:7, 12, 14–18. He pours out to God all that is in his heart. God tells him he must separate the precious from the vile in the words he speaks on God's behalf to others (15:19–21). Jeremiah can weep for the ordinary people.

Prophecies during the reign of Jehoiachin (Coniah)

Jehoiakim had been placed on the throne by Egypt after his elder brother had been dethroned and deported by Pharaoh Neco. After the battle of Carchemish, Jehoiakim was forced to become a vassal of Nebuchadnezzar, the king of Babylon. After another battle with Babylon, Egypt encouraged Judah to rebel. This was the situation that lay behind the prophecies of Jeremiah when Jehoiakim's son, Jehoiachin, or Coniah, succeeded.

In 13:18–27 Jeremiah calls on Jehoiachin and his queen to humble themselves before God. It meant accepting the yoke of Babylon and not being ensnared by Egypt into rebellion and a bid for independence.

Prophets may be unworldly, but their faith in God gives them a truer understanding of the current political situation than the ambitious politician. Verse 23 is one of the many familiar quotations.

In 22:24–30 Jeremiah prophesied that the king would die in exile. 2 Kings 24:8–16 tells how this prophecy was fulfilled. Jehoiachin's rebellion led inevitably to the Babylonian army besieging and taking the city. The royal family, nobles, and all the craftsmen, together with the treasury of palace and temple, were taken off to Babylon. The king's uncle, renamed Zedekiah, was made a vassal king in his place. Jehoiachin's reign had lasted only a hundred days!

Prophecies during the reign of Zedekiah

The people left behind in Jerusalem now blamed the exiles for all their troubles. Good riddance to bad rubbish was their attitude towards them. It is true that the king, nobles, and merchants had exploited them, but the corruption of idolatry and greed was universal. Blaming others is a self-destructive occupation.

God gave his answer to this in Jeremiah's vision of the two baskets of figs. It was not the exiles that were rubbish but those left in the city (chapter 24). The exiles would be refined in the fire of affliction, and would return, purified like gold. So Jeremiah wrote a letter to the exiles (chapter 29) telling them to accept their situation. Not only were they to settle down in Babylon, building houses and raising families, they were to 'seek the peace of the city' which had taken them captive! Then, after seventy years, God would bring them home again. Meantime, their chief task was to seek God with all their heart. Then they would find him.

Isn't this the nub of our problem? When trouble comes many seek God, but only with that small part of themselves that wants immediate relief. When relief doesn't come, they give up, and lose whatever little faith they have. But God waits. The withholding of bread is designed to test and increase our hunger. 'Keep on asking and you will receive' said Jesus, and to illustrate, he told the parables of the importunate friend (Luke 11:5–10) and the importunate widow (Luke 18:1–7).

Jeremiah also advised Zedekiah to submit to Babylon (27:12–15). The priests and prophets were saying that God would force the Babylonians to return the sacred vessels to the temple, just as he had made the Philistines return the ark. Jeremiah contradicted this belief and so came into confrontation with Hananiah (chapter 28). This experience led to his sweeping denunciation of all false prophets (23:9–40). He wept for them as they speak of visions of their own invention. Their words are like chaff, blown away by the wind. God's work is like fire and like a hammer that shatters rock.

It is easy to mistake thoughts, arising out of one's own subconscious desires and attitudes, for the word of God. False prophecy is not always a deliberate lie. This is a very relevant problem today as prophecy is being restored, along with other gifts of the Spirit. To say 'The Lord says this' without the qualification 'I believe that' can be to take God's name in vain. True vision is given to the 'pure in heart', the single-minded, to the humble-minded and obedient.

Like Isaiah, Jeremiah prophesied that judgment would fall on all the surrounding nations. In chapters 47–51 he foretells the overthrow of Philistia, Moab, Ammon, Syria and finally Babylon itself. Note in 48:11 the stale smell of those who have not experienced any suffering to disturb their ease!

The most important of Jeremiah's prophecies are those of his vision for the future. These deserve deep and careful study. He foretells the coming of a shepherd king, a righteous branch of the house of David (23:1–8), the joyful return (chapter 30) and the healing of the division of the two kingdoms (chapter 31). Ephraim is Joseph's first-born who shall return to worship God in Zion. Rachel, mother of Joseph and Benjamin, will no longer weep for her lost children. What jewels for meditation are to be found in such verses as 3 and 21.

Most important of all is the vision of a new covenant (31:31–34) quoted in Hebrews (Hebrews 8:8–10). The failure of the reform had proved to Jeremiah that the old covenant was powerless. The idea of a right spirit, that loved God from the heart, was not entirely new, but

Jeremiah made it central. It became the climax and completion of the ministry of Jesus.

To return to the history, Zedekiah was not prepared to go on submitting to Babylon. A new Pharaoh, Hophra, had come to the throne, and Zedekiah, making the same mistake as Jehoiachin, started to revive the Egyptian alliance. The result was predictable. Nebuchadnezzar renewed his attack.

Zedekiah sent Pashur to ask Jeremiah for advice (chapter 21). Jeremiah prophesied defeat, both for the city and the king, quoting the words of Deuteronomy 30:15. As always, Jeremiah's warning went unheeded. Nebuchadnezzar's army besieged the city, and Jeremiah, now regarded as a traitor, was thrown into prison (chapter 32).

Here, in prison, Jeremiah demonstrated his belief in his own prophecies. At this unlikely time, he bought a tract of family land, and handed over sealed evidence of its purchase to Baruch.

The princes now demanded Jeremiah's death, complaining that he was weakening the army's morale (chapter 38). Zedekiah allowed them to do as they pleased. Preferring not to have blood on their hands, they dumped him in a dried-up well. There he would certainly have died had not a friend, with the king's permission, rescued him. Zedekiah's relationship with Jeremiah was a bit like that of Herod and John the Baptist. He was driven to persecute a prophet he respected and half-believed in. Unlike Herod he managed to preserve Jeremiah alive, keeping him in prison largely for his own safety.

The story of the fall of the city is told in 39:1–14. Verses 15–18 are an earlier prophecy about the safety of the man who rescued him. The story is continued in chapter 52.

The aftermath   Jeremiah 40–44

All but the very poor were now taken into exile. The temple and palaces were burnt and the walls were knocked down. Jeremiah was offered the chance of going to Babylon as a free and honoured guest, but he preferred to stay and suffer with those left behind in the ruins, together with Baruch.

Gedaliah, the son of Jeremiah's great friend, had been made governor. He established some form of government at Mizpah, once Samuel's headquarters (1 Samuel 7:6) and where the kingship had originally been set up (1 Samuel 10:17–27). The tree grown rotten had been felled, but perhaps the roots were still healthy. Jeremiah and Baruch found him there.

Vain hope! Gedaliah, having learnt from experience, advised the people to submit, but Ishmael, a royal prince who had evaded capture, plotted his murder. Gedaliah refused to believe the warning he was given. As a result, he, and most of the Jews with him, were murdered. Ishmael marched off, taking as captive all the rest, including Jeremiah and Baruch. When the small forces under Gedaliah's command got news of this, they went in pursuit. The captives were rescued, but Ishmael escaped and fled. What were they to do now? Nebuchadnezzar, they thought, would surely revenge the murder of his governor. They decided to flee into Egypt, but first asked Jeremiah to seek God's guidance for them. They ask when a decision has already been made! Reluctantly Jeremiah waited ten days for God's answer. 'Stay put and I will protect you. Flee to Egypt and you will die there and never return.' Despite their oath the people refused to obey. They marched off to Egypt, taking Jeremiah and Baruch with them (chapter 42).

In Egypt the people started to worship Egyptian deities, especially Isis, or Ishtar, the queen of heaven. When Jeremiah said that such idolatry had been the cause of all their disasters, they replied that on the contrary, it was their neglect of her that had led to it. It is useless to use history to prove our beliefs to others. It is our faith that interprets history, not vice versa. However, events of history can confirm whether or not a prophecy is true.

The Book of Obadiah

When Jerusalem fell the small surrounding states showed their delight and took whatever revenge and advantage they could. Edom, the land of Esau, pounced like a jackal, and was particularly resented.

Obadiah prophesied that Edom's pride would be brought low. Zion would be delivered to repossess her possessions. He foresaw victorious exiles—'saviours'—conquering Edom and all the surrounding nations and incorporating them into a kingdom that should be the Lord's. It was a prophecy, also recorded in Daniel's vision (Daniel 2:44), which was fulfilled by Christ. Now those lands are mainly Muslim, but they still contain small Christian communities who remain faithful, despite hardship and some persecution.

Verse 17 is another bright jewel shining in a dark book.

The idea of repossessing our possessions has been used today to help Christians understand what some charismatic Christians have called the baptism of the Spirit. When we receive Christ we receive, through his Spirit, every spiritual blessing (Ephesians 1:3). It is sometimes like having a huge sum of money in the bank without knowing how to cash a cheque. How many spiritual blessings are ours, which we fail actively to possess!

The Book of Habakkuk

It has generally been believed that the prophet Habakkuk lived about 600BC when the Chaldean or Babylonian army was beginning to threaten Judah (Habakkuk 1:6). But in 1947 the Dead Sea Scrolls gave evidence that the advancing army was that of Greece, and the word Chaldean was a misinterpretation. For us, it doesn't really matter, for his basic message is timeless. It is relevant to both periods and is of great importance today. In chapter 1 Habakkuk cries out against the violence he sees advancing. If God wants to punish Judah, why does he use as his instrument a nation far more wicked and cruel? Verses 5–11 recall Isaiah's prophecy about Assyria (Isaiah 10:5–7).

Habakkuk doesn't just question God. Most of us do that. He waits for an answer. He stands, like a city watchman (Habakkuk 2:1), awaiting God's expected reproof and his own reaction to it! He did not doubt that God had an answer.

He is told to go on waiting. How important such waiting was for the prophets. The vision is delayed, but it will come. Habakkuk must be ready for it, to publish it far and wide, and as fast as possible.

Habakkuk then calls down woe on the evil aggressor. Despite the inevitable advance of evil forces, his faith in God's sovereignty is absolute (2:14). He dwells in his temple, which, as Solomon knew, was far greater than a building that could be destroyed. All sounds of fury must fade into reverent silence (2:20).

In his vision Habakkuk sees, in the advancing army, God himself coming in judgment, in glory, and in destruction. But his purpose is salvation.

As Habakkuk turns his eyes away from the enemy and fixes them on God, his natural fears, the trembling lips and churning stomach, are submerged by praise.

Only St Paul could equal his final song of triumphant faith (3:17–19; compare Romans 8:35–39).

For further reading

Psalms 40; 56; 57; 71; 88

For group discussion

1. Should parents leave the teaching of religion to their children to the Sunday School?

2. Does God give special protection to believers?

3. How does faith differ from presumption?

For private reflection

1. How would you reply to someone who complained that God made too many demands?

2. 'Blaming others is self-destruction.' What is your experience?

3. How is God's word like a fire and a hammer?

12

The Exile

Ezekiel; Isaiah 40–55

The prophet who dominated the exile was Ezekiel. He was a priest who was deported in the first wave of exiles with King Jehoiachin. We know little about him, but, in contrast to the very human and sympathetic Jeremiah, he seems austere and strange. Though many of his prophecies resemble those of the other prophets, his visionary experiences, and some of his teaching, is new and significant. His book is arranged in chronological order. No more need to skip and jump!

It is important for us to understand his situation. Jerusalem was still intact. Zedekiah had been installed by Nebuchadnezzar as a puppet king. He was being tempted to revive the Egyptian alliance and rebel. Ezekiel's call came four years before this foolish course led to final disaster.

Despite Jeremiah's warnings, the people of Jerusalem still felt secure. Blaming the exiles as the baddies, whom God had deservedly punished, they were confident God would defend his temple and city. His honour was at stake! So they continued to make hay in the last of the sunshine.

Poor God! Is his honour so bound up with institutions? When churches fall empty and are closed, when there is persecution, or a so-called Christian society falls into chaos, is this a sign that God is powerless? Poor God!

Ezekiel's visions of the glory of God   *Ezekiel 1:1—3:27*

The first need was to capture a vision of God's greatness. Their God was too small. Isaiah had a vision of God's holiness within his temple. Ezekiel, in Babylon, had a vision of his universal sovereignty. Great God!

The imagery would ring bells of deep inherited experience. The cherubim were the guardians of the mercy seat, the meeting place of God with his people (Exodus 25:20–22). Their four faces may represent four aspects of God, his love, his power, his patience and his glory. The wheels, full of eyes, show his stillness in motion. He is everywhere present, all-seeing, active and purposeful. All this imagery is also found in the visions of John in Revelation 4, together with the fire and the cloud, the throne of judgment, and the rainbow of mercy. John had certainly meditated on Ezekiel's book. Amid the glory, likened to the flashing of jewels, John too saw the likeness of a man. To describe God as a person is to limit him to human conceptions, but certainly he is personal in his dealings with us.

Ezekiel falls flat on his face, but God wants to speak to a responsible and free man. Ezekiel is told to stand up. He is called to go as a prophet to his own people. Like Isaiah, he is warned that they will not listen, but he is not to fear them. The message is to be one of love. It is seen as a scroll which he has to swallow and digest. This too is part of John's experience (Revelation 10:9–11).

As a result of this vision Ezekiel goes to the exiles by the river in Babylon. Psalm 137 describes their mood. Identifying himself with their plight, he sits with them in astonished silence for seven days. That was all very well, but to stay like that wasn't getting on with the job. God rebukes him. Ezekiel is to be as a watchman on the city wall. The city's safety depends upon him giving the warning of danger. For a watchman to fail in giving such warning is a sin. If, however, his warning is ignored, he will not be held responsible for the disaster.

Ezekiel's second vision is like the first (3:22–27). This time God tells him to be silent. He is to speak only when God opens his mouth. Prophets must not only speak the right word, but at the right time, and in the right way. That doesn't apply only to prophets!

Most Jews believed that God, like other gods, had sovereignty only within his own territory, hence Naaman's loads of earth (2 Kings 5:17–18). The exiles in Babylon felt exiled not just from their own lands, but from God. God answered their need. They would find him in Babylon or anywhere in the world they might go. His sanctuary would be within their hearts. This was the only answer to the heart's idolatry. But, to receive him, they would need to be given new hearts, which would delight to obey his commandments (11:15–25).

Again Ezekiel teaches with an acted parable. He moves house. It is a sign that soon a second wave of exiles would be joining them. He predicts that Zedekiah would go into Babylon blind (chapter 12)—which he did (2 Kings 25:7). The day of disaster, long foreseen, is now at hand.

Prophecies to Jerusalem   *Ezekiel 13:1—24:14*

Ezekiel's prophecies are now directed to the people in Jerusalem. Twice we read of delegations coming from the city to consult him (14:1; 20:1). Perhaps they hoped for better words than those given by Jeremiah. If so, they were to be disappointed.

First Ezekiel joins with Jeremiah in attacking the false prophets. 'Daubers' he calls them, slapping cement over the cracks of a tottering wall (13:1–16; also 22:23–29). Then he denounces the women exploiting people's fears by selling them amulets and charms (13:17–23). He warned the visitors against the idols in their own hearts (14:1–8). No longer could the righteousness of one man save the city. Was he, under the guise of notable heroes, referring to Jeremiah? (14:12–21; compare Genesis 18:32). The nation, says Ezekiel, has lost its only value. The vine, a popular symbol of Israel, is useful only for its fruit. As firewood, it is a dead loss. Israel had failed to fulfil her vocation. She was therefore fit only for destruction. In the next three chapters Ezekiel's message was given in a series of acted parables, designed to illustrate the siege, the famine and the destruction of Jerusalem with its inhabitants. The details of this were all so clear to him. The exiles shared the conviction of those still in Jerusalem. God would not, could not, let his city be destroyed. Not only their hope of a return to it, their very belief in God seemed to depend upon this. They had to be forewarned. Note the emphatic repetition of 'Ye shall know that I am the Lord.'

Ezekiel's vision concerning the temple   *Ezekiel 8–10*

In Ezekiel's third vision he is transported to the temple. There, a horrifying picture of idolatry is disclosed. How far these idol altars and practices were actual, which they may well have been, and how far they were the secret idolatry of the heart, is not clear (8:12).

The latter are more dangerous. Even in churches today, how many secret idols dominate the hearts of those who sing the hymns and chant the liturgies? Is God himself our chief preoccupation?

Ezekiel now understands why the temple had to be destroyed. But first, the vision shows him that those who are the true worshippers of God are to be given a distinguishing mark on their foreheads. This also is seen by John before the last seal is opened (Revelation 7:1–8). The faithful are under God's protection, though not necessarily preserved from suffering and death.

In Ezekiel's fourth vision he sees the glory of God's presence leave the temple (chapter 10). The words of Jesus show that such a departure was repeated in his day (Matthew 23:38). Nobody but he seemed to be aware of it. Would we be aware of God's absence today? If God leaves the temple where is he to be found? (See chapter 15; compare Luke 14:34–35.) It is a warning for the Church today.

Similar teaching is given in chapter 16. Using Hosea's imagery of the adulterous bride, it is a story of rags to riches, then back to rags. Judah and Samaria are like two ugly sisters. Judah has learnt nothing from her sister's fate. Note that it is their lovers, with whom they committed adultery, who destroy them. Political ambition, love of money, sensual pleasure, these things tend to destroy those who give them God's place in their lives.

Samaria is referred to as Sodom, yet Jerusalem is considered even more corrupt (16:46–52). The greater the blessing, the greater the judgment, as Jesus said of the towns he had visited (Matthew 11:20–24).

Ezekiel then denounces Zedekiah and his policy of revolt. In his parable of the two eagles (chapter 17) which represent Babylon and Egypt, he warns that he will not succeed, but will die in Babylon (17:16). The parable ends with the prophecy of a third eagle, God himself, who will replant the branch. The final words of the prophecy find echoes in the Magnificat.

Chapter 18 deals with the proverb about sour grapes. The people felt that God was punishing them unfairly for the sins of their forefathers in the time of Manassah. This would accord with the warning in the second commandment (Exodus 20:5). Ezekiel not only teaches personal responsibility, as Jeremiah had done (Jeremiah 31:29–30), he also says that judgment is pronounced on the 'now' of the present moment. He who is not faithful to the end can be lost. The penitent thief, at the last moment, can be saved. The first can be last, and the last first.

It is true that in any given situation, circumstance and psychology affect the extent of personal responsibility. We do not understand the secrets of people's hearts. We do not even understand our own, which is why we must not judge either ourselves or others. God sees the heart. He knows the extent of our responsibility, and holds us to that.

So Ezekiel calls his people to personal repentance. God will give them a new heart and a new spirit (18:31–32). He has no pleasure in the death of the wicked (18:23).

Chapter 19 is a lamentation. Alas, for the lion of Judah is snared. Alas, for the vine has been destroyed.

In the next chapter Ezekiel greets his second delegation of visitors with harshness. They want him to ask God what message he has for them? God won't even listen to them, he tells them. Why should he? They know his will and won't obey it. Note Ezekiel's priestly stress on the law of the sabbath (20:13). Other prophets had mixed feelings because of its abuse (Isaiah 1:13; Amos 5:21–24; compare Amos 8:4–5). Ezekiel sees the sabbath as a gift. It is also a sign of God's presence which makes his people holy. This isn't how it is always regarded, as the Church relates it to Sunday. But renewal begins when God is honoured and time is gladly spent, together with others, in his presence, seeking his glory and his will.

Like Hosea, Ezekiel sees God as calling them back to the wilderness. In Babylon they will repent. There, they will receive, not what they deserve, but what God, out of his love, wants to give them, his forgiveness. Ezekiel's visitors did not like his parables, no doubt complaining they couldn't understand them. They could have done, had they wanted to. To drive his point home Ezekiel becomes specific, first about the coming battle (21:1–5) then about the fate of Zedekiah (21:25–27). Finally, he gives a detailed denunciation of their social and moral sins (chapter 22). It is a familiar list. Sin is boringly repetitive. All the prophets before him had condemned them, as his hearers very well knew.

This chapter ends with a verse of great significance. Its meaning is best brought out by the Revised English Bible of 1989. 'I looked among them for a man who would build a barricade in the breach and withstand me, to avert the destruction of the land; but I found no such person.' Was Ezekiel thinking of Phinehas in Numbers 25:1–9? Psalm 106:30–31 which also refers to him is a Psalm that came out of exile. Abraham and Moses were such men (Genesis 18:23–33; Exodus 32:19–32). Where were they now? Jeremiah had prophesied, but, if it were an intercessor God was looking for, why had he told Jeremiah not to intercede (Jeremiah 7:16)? Was it then too late? We know that God does seek intercessors, and honours their prayers. In Jesus we see most perfectly the man in the breach. He is for all time our intercessor (Hebrews 7:25). We join our prayers to his.

Ezekiel now had to act out the most difficult parable of all. He was told his beloved wife would die, and he was not to weep or mourn for her. This was to be a sign to all people that the temple, which was their pride and joy, was to be destroyed, and they were not to mourn the event (24:15–27). When the news came of the city's fall, then he would be able to speak freely.

We need to jump the next eight chapters (chapters 25–32). These were added later, and contain prophecies against the small surrounding states that had rejoiced in Judah's downfall. This section also includes chapter 35, which is a denunciation of Edom similar to that of Obadiah.

In chapter 33 God repeats his calling to Ezekiel to act as a watchman. The urgency is great, the disaster imminent. The city is about to fall. The exiles' reaction, repentance or despair, will depend upon his warning.

One evening, as Ezekiel is deep in prayer, a messenger arrives. He had escaped from Jerusalem and brings news of its destruction (33:21–22). Ezekiel, mercifully, is given just one night to prepare for his meeting with the people the next morning.

A watershed has been passed. What was Ezekiel's work to be now? The tone and subject matter of his book changes. From this point on his message is one of comfort.

First, however, Ezekiel had to learn something about himself. During those days of shocked discovery, he had to reassert that the disaster was the consequence of disloyalty to God. The message he had previously targeted to the people of Jerusalem, he now had to repeat for the benefit of the exiles. He was now released to speak to them freely.

Then came another shock of discovery. The people flocked to hear him. He was apparently popular and a great success. He was an eloquent speaker, and they enjoyed his sermons. But these made not the slightest difference to their lives. Ezekiel, to his dismay, found himself regarded as a provider of free entertainment! (33:30–32).

God had deprived Ezekiel of what he may have regarded as his greatest talent. God had good reason. Moses was no speaker (Exodus 4:10); neither was St Paul (1 Corinthians 2:1–4). Paul discovered that God's strength is made perfect in weakness (2 Corinthians 12:9). Words are easily forgotten. How many sermons do we remember? Even last week's easily fades. But actions, especially those as dramatic as Ezekiel's acted parables, stick in the mind. Eloquent preachers can fill churches, that empty again when they depart, demonstrating the emptiness of their oratory. A church has often been filled by a minister self-effacing and entirely devoid of a speaker's skills. The Spirit works through his love and prayer.

Visions of the future   *Ezekiel 34–48*

The second wave of exiles now began to arrive. Among them were the two chief priests and three Levites, as well as Zedekiah's army commander. The king of Babylon had all of them put to death (2 Kings 25:18–21).

Chapter 34 leads off with an attack on false shepherds who have fed themselves rather than the flock. Ezekiel prophesies that God will come as a shepherd to his people. First he sees God himself shepherding them out of Babylon, as Moses had shepherded them out of Egypt. In verses 23–25, however, he speaks of God setting up one shepherd, a prince of the house of David. His coming will pave the way for a new covenant. Jesus must surely have meditated on these verses which he came to fulfil (John 10:1–16).

Ezekiel prophesies not just a return but a restoration. Cities will be rebuilt. They will be repopulated by people cleansed from sin and given a new heart and spirit (36:8–10, 25–27). They will be a holy flock, a witness to the surrounding nations of God's salvation. It will be Eden restored (verses 33–38).

Now follows Ezekiel's great vision of the valley of dry bones. For most Christians it is the only thing they know about Ezekiel. It has been made famous by song. What a dramatic picture of the dead coming to life, and the Spirit blowing to bring the nation to new birth. Ezekiel has the double task of prophesying to the bones, and calling for the Spirit.

He then acts out one more parable. He binds together two sticks.

Israel and Judah will be restored as one united nation. Ezekiel 37:15–22 is a favourite reading for services concerned with Church unity.

Chapters 38–39 look further into the future, to a time when Gentile nations will again gather together against the land of Israel. This was partly fulfilled when the Greek King Antiochus Epiphanes conquered and desecrated the Temple with an altar to Zeus in 167BC. Again, it was partly fulfilled when the Romans destroyed the city in AD70.

Gog and Magog are mysterious figures who reappear in Revelation (Revelation 20:7–15). They will lead a final assault on the holy city which will usher in the last judgment. These chapters influence the minds of many people today, who see in present events an approach to their final fulfilment.

Chapters 40–48 contain Ezekiel's vision of the temple to be. The description is very detailed, and became a blueprint for those who later did the rebuilding. But there is far more to it than that. Ezekiel sees God's glory returning to it (43:1–5). Precautions are taken to ensure that it will never again be polluted (chapter 44). Verse 9 explains the violence met by St Paul (Acts 21:26–31). Verse 25 explains the action of priest and Levite in Jesus' parable. The priestly Ezekiel sees a *cordon sanitaire* drawn between the sacred and the secular.

Chapters 45 and 46 deal with the restoration of the sacrifices and the worship, but in chapter 47 there is the wonderful vision of the river of life (verses 1–12). Here is a source of profound meditation.

So many of the images in this chapter are found in St John's vision of the holy city (Revelation 21–22): its measurements (Ezekiel 40:1–3, 47; Revelation 21:15–17); the presence of God's glory (Revelation 21:22–23); the exclusion of all that pollutes (Revelation 21:27); the river of life (Revelation 22:1–2); the gates named after the twelve tribes (Ezekiel 48:31; Revelation 21:12); finally, the name of the city, 'The Lord is there' (Ezekiel 48:35; Revelation 21:3). This vision still shines for us today.

Scripture, synagogue and sabbath

The major concern of any group of exiles, once their physical survival is assured, is the survival of their religious and cultural identity.

For the first time since leaving Egypt, the Jews were surrounded by races of alien beliefs and customs and a civilization more sophisticated than their own. They had to stress the things that made them different, or they would be absorbed into the mish-mash and lose for ever the special purpose of their existence.

The priests and Levites had carried with them into exile their scrolls of sacred writings. These included books of the Law, histories, royal records, collections of stories, songs, psalms, proverbs and prophecies. It was the literature of a nation, summarizing the totality of their experience.

Their first urgent task was to rethink and interpret this experience in the light of recent catastrophic events. They had plenty of time for this. With the help of scribes, the priests, and Levites collected the different historical records, such as the two known as *J* and *E* from their use of different words for God—*Jehovah*—or rather *Yahweh*—(translated 'The LORD') and *Eloi* (translated 'God'). Their added interpretation, fairly easy to recognize, is known by biblical scholars as *P* (priestly). As result of the work of the priests and Levites, the Old Testament books came into being, though later more books were written and added.

Because they believed their exile was a punishment for their disobedience to God's Law, it was very important that the Law should be taught to the people. Lacking the temple, sacrifices could not be offered, but, as God was still with them, worship could. So synagogues were set up. Here Psalms were sung and prayers said, but the most important activity was the reading of the Law. Priests and Levites became important as teachers and interpreters.

It was not practically possible to keep all the Law. Emphasis was laid on those laws that kept the Jews separate, the law of the sabbath, the rules about food, and the rite of circumcision. These still distinguish the Jewish community today.

The prophet of the return   *Isaiah 40–55*

Towards the end of the period of exile there arose another voice proclaiming God's word. The voice is nameless but his prophecies are found in the Book of Isaiah, chapters 40–55. He is referred to as Second Isaiah. These prophecies clearly relate to the years just before the return from exile, two generations later than the time of Isaiah of Jerusalem. But their author, or possibly authors, echo much of his teaching, and stem from his tradition. A new force was appearing on the political horizon. Cyrus the Mede was building up a new Persian Empire to become the largest ever known. Asia Minor, Greece and Egypt had toppled. Next in line was Babylon.

The Persians were very different. Cyrus was a Zoroastrian, the religion of the prophet Zarathusta, now followed by the Parsees. Like the Jews, they believed in one God, whose chief requirement was ethical. Life is a conflict between good and evil forces: God and the devil. God will ultimately triumph. Salvation in an after-life depends on aligning oneself in this life with the good.

Cyrus' policy towards the deportation of every nation he found scattered by previous empires was to send them all home. Second

Isaiah believed that not only would Cyrus overthrow Babylon, but he would be the saviour God had promised to raise up, to set his people free to return.

For First Isaiah to see Assyria as God's instrument of punishment was one thing. To see Cyrus, a non-Jew, as a saviour and call him 'God's beloved' was another. It must have sent shock waves throughout the community.

This 'Book of Comfort' as it has been called, starts with the words 'Comfort ye', made famous by Handel's *Messiah*. The first chapter sums up the teaching of the book, and is one of the most beautiful chapters in the whole of the Old Testament. This is a book for meditation rather than explanation. Here, however, is a summary of its leading themes.

There is only one God, creator of all the world. Other gods and idols are not rivals. They are nothings. Earlier prophets had glimpses of this truth, but ordinary Jews believed the God of Israel was one amongst many, though, of course, superior, a King of all gods (Psalm 95:3). In this book we find the first full proclamation of monotheism.

God had called Cyrus. He is 'the righteous man' (41:2 AV), 'my shepherd' (44:28), God's 'anointed' (45:1–4, 13). The Jews never accepted what was implied by this. Even Peter got a shock when he saw how God had accepted the Roman Cornelius (Acts 10:34–35). There are Christians today who would find it hard to believe God could anoint and use a Hindu.

The exiles were called to be the returning remnant. The journey would pass through the desert and be dangerous, but God would protect them. He would provide a highway for them (40:3–4; compare 35:8–10). He would supply them with water (Isaiah 41:17–20), and with light in the darkness (42:16), as he had in their wanderings with Moses. He would bring them safely across rivers as well as deserts (43:1–2). He would even carry them (40:11; 46:4). They would go out in joy and peace (48:20; 51:11; 55:12).

They are a people loved, forgiven and restored (40:1–2; 43:2–5; 44:22). Their trials have been a refining process (48:10). Their names are engraved upon God's hands (49:16). His covenant with them is everlasting (54:10).

God's purpose is that they should be his witnesses to the Gentiles. This was implicit in Abraham's call, but had never been accepted (43:10, 21; 45:21–22). They were to show forth God's salvation and his praise (43:21; compare 1 Peter 2:9).

This commission is made especially clear in the four servant songs (42:1–4; 49:1–12; 50:4–10; 52:13—53:12). These four mysterious prophecies belong together. Who was this suffering servant? Some have thought the original model to have been Jeremiah. Some see it as a picture of the whole Jewish race, whose history of suffering has continued up to our own day. But, when the Ethiopian asked Philip this question (Acts 8:27–35), Philip pointed him to Jesus Christ.

Jeremiah had spoken of a coming Messiah, an anointed king of the house of David, who would be a saviour and righteous judge, all symbols of earthly power. This was the kind of Messiah the Jews came to expect. Jesus was unique in seeing these prophecies of a suffering servant as belonging to the Messiah. They determined the path he was to follow. They took him to the cross. This way of suffering love, this victory through death, is what chiefly divides the Christian faith from that of the Muslim as well as the Jew.

The message of this nameless prophet went largely unheeded in his own time. It was to be the inspiration behind the books of Ruth and Jonah. Since its fulfilment by Christ, it speaks to his Church, the new Israel, now called to be his witnesses to all the world, proclaiming the 'meekness and majesty' of God. This 'Book of Comfort' inspires and strengthens us in our own spiritual journey.

For further reading

Revelation 1; 4; 21; 22; Psalm 22; 1 Corinthians 1:18–31; Hebrews 12:18–29

For group discussion

1. How can the Church make greater use of acted stories? Think of some modern parable you could act.

2. Should a distinction be drawn between the sacred and the secular? If so, where?

3. What is the proper place of a sermon in our worship? Do we make it too central?

For private reflection

1. Is your God too small?

2. How does God use your strengths and your weaknesses?

3. Do you see prayer as a barricade to avert the destruction of our land?

13

Return of the Remnant

Haggai; Zechariah 1–8; Malachi; Isaiah 56–66

In 593BC Cyrus overthrew the Babylonian Empire and decreed that all deported people could return home. Jeremiah had predicted that the exile would last seventy years. In fact it lasted sixty for the first batch of exiles and fifty for the second.

He had told the exiles to settle down, to build houses and marry wives. The object of deportation had not been primarily to enslave them, but to prevent the conquered people rising in rebellion. So the Jews, as they were now called, did settle, and, with their industry and talent for trading and making money, many of them became rich. Some married Babylonian wives, and even worshipped Babylonian gods.

So it isn't surprising that there wasn't any widespread enthusiasm for a return. It meant uprooting, taking a long and dangerous desert journey, to find what? An empty city, with hardly a house left standing, amid fields and orchards run wild and overgrown, and surrounded by unfriendly aliens as neighbours. The comfortable majority opted to stay put. Like Esau, they were willing to sell their birthright, but for rather more than a bowl of lentils. As all the prophets predicted, only a faithful remnant returned home.

Between 538–520BC they began to straggle back. It seems they started to try and rebuild the temple, but the effort was too great. All their energy was taken up in rebuilding their own houses, clearing the fields, and replanting crops. As for the temple, 'We'll get around to it sometime' was their attitude. This 'sometime' was continuously postponed, until, in 520BC, another prophet thundered in their ears.

The Book of Haggai

The book of Haggai is now used mostly to provide a suitable reading for churches wanting to raise money for building restoration. Fair enough. That is exactly what Haggai was talking about. Haggai points out that putting our own needs first may sound reasonable but it is, in fact, a recipe, not for prosperity, but for disaster (chapter 1).

Today we might not make such a simple connection between materialistic greed, religious indifference and drought, but, with a growing awareness of ecology, we are becoming increasingly aware that a connection is there. It is not just a matter of science, either. There is also a mysterious linkage between the forces of nature and man (Romans 8:19–32). Do we, for instance, believe that rain will fall in answer to prayer? When this happens, as it has often done, do we just call it coincidence? Would we say this of the healing of a sick person, when prayer has been made? If rain does not always fall, neither are all the sick healed. Prayer is not like a slot machine, ensuring an automatic response in our favour.

Within twenty-four days the work was started, but within a month, the people were again disheartened. So Haggai calls upon Zerubbabel, the governor, and Joshua, the high priest, to be strong and complete the work (chapter 2). The task is urgent, for God will fill the temple with his glory. Then all nations will come to worship him, bringing him their offerings. Such a temple will outshine that of Solomon. When people respond in faith, God will provide the wherewithal. This is the experience of countless ventures of faith through the ages. Ours too perhaps.

Haggai goes on to predict that Zerubbabel would prove to be the longed-for Messiah. He was in fact royal, being a descendent of David (1 Chronicles 3:1–19). Haggai, however, was wrong. His temple also was not to be the temple of God's glory. It was destroyed by the Greeks, rebuilt by Herod, and again destroyed by the Romans. Both Haggai's prophecies were fulfilled only by Jesus Christ. He was the Messiah. His body was the temple, destroyed and raised in three days to become the temple which is his body, the Church (John 2:19–21; Ephesians 2:19–22).

The prophet Zechariah   *Zechariah 1–8*

The prophet Zechariah lived at the same time as Haggai. His prophecies between the years 520–517BC are found in the first eight chapters of his book. The rest of the chapters belong to a later period.

In 522BC all the subject states of the Persian Empire were in revolt, and the Jews lived in a state of hope and expectation. It was rather like that of Eastern Europe, as Communist rule started to collapse. A golden age seemed to be round the corner. The Jews believed that the reign of the Messiah was imminent, and his kingdom would, as prophesied, restore their freedom and independence, and bring in an age of peace and unparalleled prosperity. It was this that gave Zechariah his source of urgency for the completion of the temple. It had to be ready for the Messiah when he came. The same urgency lies behind the call for a Decade of Evangelism today.

Zechariah's book starts with a call to repentance (Zechariah 1:1–6). Then follow eight visions.

The four horsemen (1:7–17). These are the spirits of God patrolling the earth. The vision gives the assurance that God has returned to Jerusalem, and his temple will be built.

The four horns and four carpenters (1:18–21). This foretells the overthrow of the Gentile powers. Though Jerusalem had a descendent of David as its governor, it was still under Persian control.

The man with the measuring line (chapter 2). The city is not to be measured, or enclosed with a wall. It is to be open to peoples of every nation who will be drawn to worship there. God himself will be as a wall of fire around the city, and a glory within. Here is a vision of the heavenly Jerusalem seen by John (Revelation 21). Zechariah believed it would be true of the earthly city of his own day.

The clothing of Joshua (chapter 3). *Satan* in Hebrew, is a word meaning 'Accuser'. Satan would like God's people to be paralysed by a sense of guilt. He is rebuked. Joshua is to put off clothes of mourning for the past. He, as representative of his people, has been saved and purified by the fire of suffering. Now he is reclothed in new and glorious robes, a restored and holy priest, set over God's new house. He is to be ready to receive the Branch, the anointed king, the Messiah, foretold by Jeremiah (Jeremiah 23:5–6).

We have seen that Haggai believed the Branch was Zerubbabel, and Zechariah would no doubt have shared this belief. Why, then, do the verses 11–13 of chapter 6 refer to Joshua? It is very probable that Joshua's name was substituted for that of Zerubbabel in the light of later events. When independence was finally gained, after the war with Greece, the high priests became kings. This would account for the alteration made by a scribe. Jesus fulfilled the prophecy by being both king and priest, after the order of Melchizedek (Hebrews 7:17–21). His was a new and unique priesthood for a new and unique sacrifice.

The candlestick with seven lamps (chapter 4). This is the Menorah, now a symbol of Israel. Here is a picture of the Spirit of God, through whose power alone Zerubbabel will be able to do the work for which he is called (compare Revelation 4:5). The oil flows in continuous supply from two olive trees, through two branches. For Zechariah these two branches were Zerubbabel and Joshua. For John (Revelation 11:1–12) they were to be God's prophets and witnesses in the last days of persecution. Zechariah's vision is a wonderful encouragement to us all. Empowered by the Spirit we will not despise small beginnings. The gospel planted like a mustard seed now has branches that have spread all over the globe.

The flying scroll (5:1–4) is a picture of all the wickedness of the city being searched out and destroyed by a curse.

The ephah and the woman (5:5–11) depicts wickedness itself, in a measuring basket, being flown out of the city like an unwanted immigrant, and dumped in Babylon. Today, some may object to this portrayal of sin as a woman. Ever since the garden of Eden, women have been blamed as the cause of all wickedness. Zechariah's vision certainly influenced John, who saw Babylon as the harlot, the scarlet woman, but for him, Babylon was a synonym disguising Rome, the city of seven hills (Revelation 17). The devil is usually pictured as a man, which perhaps makes things fair. The Church is also seen as a woman, Christ's beautiful bride.

The four chariots (chapter 6). A holy priesthood, a holy people, and a holy city, will now be ready for the crowning of the Messiah. He will sit on his throne, with his priest beside him. The Jewish exiles from the northern kingdom, expelled by Assyria, will also return and they will build the temple together.

The last two chapters, (Zechariah 7–8) answer the people's question about the fast days they had been observing. There were four of them, days of mourning for the beginning of the siege of Jerusalem, the breaking of the walls, the destruction of the temple, and the murder of Gedaliah. Was there any longer a need to continue such fasts? The answer is a decisive 'No' (8:19). What God wants is truth and mercy (7:9; 8:3), peace (8:16) and joy (8:19).

Zechariah ends with a prophecy that the Gentiles will flock to this restored and holy city. The witness to which the Jews are called is the attraction of a holy life (8:18–23).

The despondent generation

The temple was rebuilt but the Persian Empire was not overthrown. Zerubbabel wasn't the Messiah. The messianic age did not dawn. When hopes are raised and then dashed, despondency takes over, even cynicism.

Some Jews returned to serving idols, others to serving their own interests. The Law was disregarded, the sabbath ignored, and the usual sins of social injustice and immorality were indulged in. Those who hung on to religious observance performed the rituals, but their hearts were not in them. Boredom set in.

God had promised never to abandon his people. Now he raised up two more prophets to challenge them and renew their hope: Malachi and the author of the last eleven chapters of Isaiah.

The Book of Malachi

We don't know the prophet's name. *Malachi* simply means 'Messenger'. Writing in the middle of the fifth century BC, he uses the form of dialogue. God answers the muttered questions lying behind the people's discontent.

'This so-called loving God, what has he done for us?' It's easy enough to forget our own past mercies. As for those of our forefathers, we feel no gratitude at all. A Jewish boy was taught to honour his father. No such honour was shown to God. Offerings of the unwanted, the second-rate, sixpence in the bag, that, they thought, was good enough for God, together with a bored yawn. They wouldn't dare to show their governor such disrespect. It would shock the Gentiles, as lack of reverence in some Christians today shocks Hindus and Muslims, every aspect of whose lives are bound up with their devotion.

Malachi then turns on the priests. First he draws an ideal picture of the early priests, Godfearing, preachers of truth, patterns of goodness, justice and peace. Were they really like this, or did distance give them a holy glow? It is now Malachi who asks the questions. If God created us to be one family, why all this partiality, in-fighting and social distinction (2:1–10)? He attacks their idolatry, their insincere prayers, and their unfaithfulness to their wives. If they are bored with God, God is bored with them. In how many churches today are men and women honoured and elected on to church councils because they are rich or powerful, while their infidelities or questionable business practices are overlooked?

The people are disheartened because their Messiah did not come. Malachi now warns them that, when he does come, they won't like him. He will come with a judgment of fire, to refine them painfully like gold. God does not change, and neither does his purpose of salvation. These words were recalled and preached by John the Baptist (Matthew 3:11). Jesus himself acted them out when he cleared the money-changers out of the temple. John puts this incident at the beginning of his ministry, so it would come as an extra shock (John 2:13–17).

Malachi then calls on the people to give God the tithes commanded by the Law. This may sound like a rather tame conclusion to what has gone before. It's fair however, to ask how many Christians give God a tenth of their income? It isn't possible to measure a person's devotion by the amount they put on the plate, as Jesus made clear in his comments on the widow's mite, but, incomes being equal, the two are not unrelated.

Malachi now comes to the question lying at the heart of the problem: 'What profit is there in serving God?' (3:14–15). The proud prosper, the wicked flourish. The practice of religion seems a waste of time. Malachi gives no answer to this. Argument would not convince. Instead, he observes that small groups of worshippers were meeting to share their faith with each other. God had noted their names, and valued them as his jewels. In the day of judgment he will keep them secure.

The book ends with Malachi's famous prophecy of the day of the Lord, when the sun of righteousness would come with healing in his wings (4:2). Zechariah sang of this in his song known as the Benedictus (Luke 1:78). The occasion was the naming of his son John. It was this John that Jesus recognized as his forerunner, the prophesied second Elijah (4:4–6; compare Mark 9:11–13).

Third Isaiah   *Isaiah 56–66*

In these chapters we hear another anonymous voice. Its echoes and points of resemblance to the other two Isaiahs have led to its inclusion in this book. It contains two very different messages, so different that some scholars think there may be two voices we hear, not one. The first voice has close links with that of Malachi. It starts with a call to obey the Law, and insists on the keeping of the sabbath (Isaiah 56:1–2). It attacks complacency (56:9–12), social injustice (57:1; 59:2–15) and adultery (57:3–4). In denouncing idolatry it refers to the horrific human sacrifices made to the Babylonian God Marduk which took place in the Valley of Hinnom just outside the city (57:5). It rebukes religious boredom (57:10) and meaningless fasts (58:1–6). Some Lenten fasts can be like this, as when smoking is given up, leading to six weeks of nervy bad temper, followed by a resumption of the habit on Easter Day!

True fasting is described, together with the true keeping of the sabbath (58:7–14). The true temple is one that is open to all who love and serve God. This should include eunuchs, previously shut out by the Law (Deuteronomy 23:1), and foreigners, who had adopted the Jewish faith, accepted the Law and been circumcised (56:4–8). Here is a hint of further outreach still, echoed by Jesus' words about his 'other sheep' (John 10:16). This vision culminates in the words quoted by Jesus to condemn the traffickers in the temple, (56:7; compare Luke 19:46).

Another voice, perhaps, seems to sound in 57:13–21. Where is God? Not just in the temple, but in the high and holy place, beyond time and space. Yet he stoops to enter the hearts of humble men and women. This was the great discovery of the exile. The fruit of such an experience is true peace, and there is a quotation from Isaiah of the exile (Isaiah 48:22; 57:21).

As God looks upon the evil state into which his people had again so quickly fallen, he wonders that there was no intercessor (59:16). This takes up the vision Ezekiel had of God searching for a man to stand in the breach (Ezekiel 22:30). Finding no one, God decides to come himself. Donning the heavenly armour (compare Ephesians 6:13–17) he will come in the power of the Spirit as the 'redeemer' of Zion. This is no earthly Messiah, a role Zerubbabel had been cast for, and had failed to fulfil. This was God himself, coming as Messiah to overcome the forces of evil. What a wonderful promise is given in 59:19. It is for all time, and has inspired generations of Christians in dark days. It is a battlecry for us, facing the unleashed evils of today.

The Jews of Jesus' day were looking for a more successful Zerubbabel, so they didn't recognize Jesus as he fulfilled this prophecy by combining it with the earlier prophecies of the suffering servant. The insight was too profound. The triumphant vision was seen again by John, as he saw the Word of God riding to final victory (Revelation 19:11–16).

What glorious chapters now follow. When the day of God's Messiah comes, the Gentiles will come to God's light. God will accept them, and they too will help to build the city of God. The words that open chapter 60, set gloriously to music by Handel, not only point forward to Jesus' birth at Bethlehem, but to his final coming. The vision in Isaiah 60–62 is identical to that of Revelation 21–22.

Chapter 61 starts with the proclamation read by Jesus at the start of his ministry, 'This day is this scripture fulfilled,' he said (Luke 4:16–21). It is a message of joy, and it leads to joyful worship and praise of God, the source of all joy. What a contrast to the boredom!

In chapter 62 the land is to be renamed, as Hosea's children were renamed. 'Hephzibah' means 'Delight in her'. 'Beulah' means 'married'. The land is God's bride, his own beloved.

The prophet has therefore a sense of urgency. The watchman is no longer set to warn the people of disaster. He is to alert them to the coming of their bridegroom. We join the saints in their cry, 'Even so, come, Lord Jesus' (Revelation 22:20). In the meantime, like John the Baptist, we are called to 'cast up the highway, gather out the stones, and lift up a standard for the people'. This is exactly what 'marching for God' is aiming to do in our land today.

In the last four chapters we come back to earth with a bump, to wretchedness and sin.

Isaiah 63:1–6 refers to the punishment of Edom (compare Obadiah). Note once again, God's astonishment that there were no intercessors to uphold, as Aaron and Hur upheld the prayerful arms of Moses. There is deep thanksgiving for God's continuing loving kindness, and a picture of God as a saviour, who shares in the suffering of his people. This was certainly true of Jesus. Many theologians deny that there is suffering in the heart of God. 'God', they say, 'cannot feel.' All words that we apply to God are utterly inadequate. Being human, we can only use words that have human application, and God is beyond what is human. But he is not less than human. In Jesus we see God's image (Colossians 1:15) expressed in human terms that we can understand. Let that be enough for us. We do not need to argue abstractions, or quibble over words.

How pitifully far were these despondent people from the faith of Abraham. Would he be able to recognize them as his descendants? John the Baptist shared their doubts (Matthew 3:9). So did Jesus (John 8:37–44). So did Paul (Romans 2:28–29). But God our Father, our creator, in spite of our miserable rags, which includes our so-called 'righteousness' (64:6), will never fail to recognize his children when, like the prodigal, they return to him. The plaintive cry ringing out in this chapter is the old exclusive cry against their alien neighbours of mixed race. The Gentiles are the enemy who destroyed the temple. They are the outsiders.

In chapter 64 the prophet cries out with his people for God to come down from heaven to save them. Again we hear echoes of Malachi. Their worship and their religious practices are nothing but sin. Using Jeremiah's imagery of God as a potter, they pray that he will remould and not cast them away.

Chapter 65 is God's reply. The people who are truly spreading their hands towards God are the Gentiles. As for the people of Jerusalem, the shoe is on the other foot. They complain God does not listen to their prayers. In fact, it is God who has been spreading out his hands to them, in vain. It is they who will not listen. They are idolaters. They break the dietary laws, yet, like the Pharisees in Jesus' day, they stink with self-righteousness. As from the beginning, a curse will fall on those who will not answer when God calls (65:12). To be called is a heavy responsibility!

For those who say 'Yes' to God, there will be joy (65:14). The chapter ends with the promise of a totally new creation, and a new Jerusalem, a city and a people of joy. The promise of prosperity and peace recalls the vision of First Isaiah (Isaiah 11:6–9). Never accuse God of being deaf, when the promise of verse 24 is there to grasp. It is his Spirit who plants the prayer in our hearts. His answer is ready, waiting for us to stretch out with faith to receive it (Romans 8:26; Mark 11:24).

The last chapter recapitulates the themes of the previous chapters. Those who feared and loved God, and who evidently were facing rejection and some persecution, are promised that, when the Lord comes they will rejoice (66:5).

But the book ends with a terrible warning which Jesus quoted (Mark 9:48). Hell is a reality to be reckoned with.

For further reading

Psalms 96; 100; 134; 2 Corinthians 9; 2 Peter 3:1–14

For group discussion

1. What is the cause and result of a lack of a sense of urgency in our Church? How can it be revived?

2. Why do so many Christians find church services boring?

3. Does our giving reflect our faith?

For private reflection

1. How is guilt Satan's substitute for repentance?

2. What causes despondency? How do we cope with it?

3. Is joy a feeling or something deeper? What is its source?

14

Building Walls for the Last Days

Nehemiah; Ezra; 1 and 2 Chronicles; Joel; Zechariah 9–14

A dispirited nation needs more than prophets to rebuke and give visions of the future. It needs an inspired leader who can unite and galvanize his people into action. Such a man was Nehemiah.

The Book of Nehemiah

Nehemiah is an exciting book. Written about 300BC by a Levite, drawing upon Nehemiah's own memories, it is the story of a man who, with prayer, courage and determination, completed the difficult task God gave him, the rebuilding of the walls of Jerusalem.

Just as the story of Abraham can throw light on our own spiritual pilgrimage, so Nehemiah's battle with forces of opposition can encourage us in our spiritual warfare.

Chapter 1 tells how the challenge came. He was cup bearer to the king of Persia, Artaxerxes I. This would date his call 445BC. While serving the king in the palace of Susa, the Persian capital, his brother Hanani, one of the returned exiles, visited him, and gave him news of the ruined state of the city.

Note the details of Nehemiah's response. Tears and mourning are succeeded by fasting and prayer. His appeal to God is based on confidence in God's faithfulness. He identifies himself with his people and confesses his own sins as well as theirs. Taking his stand on God's promises, he pleads for them. He ends his prayer with a very specific request. Then he waits for God to answer, and open up an opportunity for action.

Nehemiah waits four months (1:1; 2:1)—four months of continuous prayer and expectancy. Then how wonderfully God rewards him by providing a truly God-given opening. The king himself raised the subject by asking a question. Then it is the king himself who asks Nehemiah to make a request. All Nehemiah has to do is offer up an arrow prayer before replying. Note that he has a clear answer to give, together with a carefully prepared and detailed plan. The king grants all he asks, and Nehemiah gives all the praise to God.

Nehemiah set out for Jerusalem with an armed guard to protect him on the journey. He also had letters from the king appointing him as governor of the city, with a mandate to restore it, and rebuild its walls.

The situation confronting him was difficult. Jerusalem was part of a district governed by Sanballat. He was a non-Jew, and would resent any loss of his authority. He would certainly resist any resurgence of Jewish power.

The land had been settled by a mixture of races placed there by the Assyrians after the deportation. These Samaritans, as they came to be called, had intermarried with the Jews, adopting some of the Jewish beliefs and practices, but mixing them up with their own. The Jewish nobles, concerned only with their own peace and prosperity, did not want to provoke Sanballat's hostility. The priests, too, could not be relied upon. Eliashib, the high priest, had a grandson married to Sanballat's daughter (13:28).

Nehemiah can trust no one but his brother. Secretly, by night, he surveys the city walls. Then he summons the nobles and tells them he has come, with royal authority, to rebuild the walls. With this assurance, and given no time to discuss the matter between themselves, they agree to start the work (chapter 2).

Sanballat's first reaction is scorn. Were they planning war against the Persian Empire? Nehemiah more or less tells him to mind his own business. Jerusalem is God's.

So the work begins. It is divided between different groups, each with corporate responsibility. At first all seem eager, except for the nobles of Tekoa (3:5). There was a danger however, that their apathy might reflect the secret feeling of the other nobles.

As the wall progressed, so Sanballat's opposition mounted: mockery turned to sneers of contempt. How could a wall be built out of a heap of rubble? The workers were a bunch of bumbling amateurs, attempting the impossible. Nehemiah answered this attempt to undermine morale, with prayer. The people took heart and the work progressed (4:1–6).

When it reached the half-way mark, Sanballat took action. He got together a number of people, hostile to the Jews, and planned an attack. Again, Nehemiah prayed, but he also organized defence. While half the people worked, the other half were to stand guard. A trumpeter was set to give the alarm. Nehemiah could then direct all to the point of surprise attack. Everyone was to sleep inside the city, clothed and on red alert. As a result of all this, the planned attack was called off (4:7–23).

Nehemiah's next problem came from division within his own ranks. To pay the Persian king's taxes, the poorer people had been forced to borrow money from the nobles. In doing so, they had pledged land, houses, and finally themselves as bond slaves. When Nehemiah learnt of this he was enraged. He called a public meeting and ordered the nobles to disgorge. He was in a strong moral position to do this. He had refused to be paid, or fed at the people's expense, and had renounced all a governor's usual perks of office. He had even fed a large number of people at his own expense (chapter 5).

Nehemiah's plea that God would remember all that he had done, and reward him, is a repeated refrain. If we find him smug, we need to remember that the belief that salvation is by grace, not works, depends on Christ. Nehemiah's cry is that of a lonely and hard-pressed man. It is recorded in the secrecy of his private memoirs.

When all but the gates is completed, Sanballat plots murder. Blandly he invites Nehemiah to meet him for consultation in a nearby village. Nehemiah refuses such distraction. His singlemindedness saves his life (6:1–4).

Sanballat's next ploy was a threat of reporting him to the Persian king as having royal ambitions for himself. Nehemiah denies this, and resorting again to prayer, successfully called Sanballat's bluff. Sanballat didn't write. False accusation can boomerang. Nehemiah's relationship with the king had been close, and one of trust (6:5–9).

The final attack was devious. It was an effort of character assassination. Nehemiah was to be warned of a plot to murder him, and, being persuaded to seek refuge in the temple, would be shown up as a coward. Nehemiah saw through the plot. His reply was proudly magnificent (6:11).

So the wall was finished. Nehemiah's enemies were cast down, and forced to recognize God's hand in it. Nehemiah's most dangerous enemies had not been Sanballat and his minions, but the quislings among his own nobles. These had leaked and carried reports to and from Tobiah. If Sanballat is the wolf in this story, then Tobiah is the jackal. Tobiah was an Ammonite, married to a Jewess. He was also a friend of the high priest, who, as we have seen, was himself allied by marriage to Sanballat.

Nehemiah now handed over his office as governor to his brother. He had promised the king that he would return to Susa by a fixed date, and he kept his promise. During his absence the high priest gave Tobiah a home in rooms within the temple court. When Nehemiah returned and discovered this, he was furious. Like Moses, he had a temper! He rejected Tobiah, throwing out all his household stuff into the courtyard. Then he had all the rooms ritually fumigated. It must have been quite a scene! (13:4–9).

But the rot did not end there. Tithes had not been collected, so the Levites, left unpaid, had given up their duties in the temple and gone off to tend their fields. Nehemiah dealt with this problem too (13:10–14).

He also discovered that foreign traders were entering the city to sell on the sabbath. Nehemiah ordered the gates to be closed from sundown of sabbath eve until the morning after the sabbath was over. The traders then took to camping just outside the walls. As darkness fell, many Jews hooked up their wares in baskets. Nehemiah had to drive the traders still further away (13:15–22).

Worst of all was the intermarriage which had become common. Children of such marriages often couldn't even speak Hebrew, let alone know about their faith. Sanballat couldn't make Nehemiah loose his cool. It was the persistent faithlessness of his own people that made him curse and swear (13:25).

The Book of Ezra

In outlining the Book of Nehemiah the reader will have noticed that several chapters have been skipped. Chapter 8 introduces the character of Ezra, and this raises problems both about his book and its chronology.

It makes a nice question for theological students, 'Who came to Jerusalem first, Ezra or Nehemiah?' Nehemiah 8:9 states that they were there together. Comparing Ezra 7:7 with Nehemiah 2:1 it appears that Ezra came there first. But a more likely possibility is that he came there fifty years later. The only certainty we have is that Nehemiah was active in Jerusalem from 445–433BC.

Persian kings were not original in their choice of names for their successor. There were two kings called Darius, two called Ahazuerus, and two called Artaxerxes. The Chronicler, who wrote both books, does not give the kings their numbers. No solution fits all the facts. Written more than a century later, the Chronicler is not to be relied on for accuracy. That was not his interest. But, if it is accepted that Nehemiah came to Jerusalem in the reign of Artaxerxes I (445BC), and Ezra came in the reign of Artaxerxes II (398BC), forty-seven years later, the events seem to fall into place and make the most sense.

As in the case of Nehemiah, the Chronicler was able to make use of contemporary memoirs. Those of Ezra provide some vivid insight into the man and his work. This was to restore the Law, a mission he pursued with passionate zeal.

His book begins where 2 Chronicles ends. It is in fact a sequel by the same author. Chapter 1 describes how Cyrus issued his proclamation, allowing the Jews to return home, taking with them whatever still remained of their temple vessels.

As we have seen, there was no immediate large-scale response. The main exodus under Zerubbabel, which is described in chapter 2, took place fifteen years later. It is unlikely that the feast of Tabernacles was held at that time (3:4). It was held later, at the time of Ezra, when it was looked on as unique (Nehemiah 8:13–17). But work on the temple was started amid great rejoicing (Ezra 3:8–13). Then it was abandoned.

The reason given by Haggai was apathy. The Book of Ezra suggests another reason. When the work began, the people of the land, the Samaritans, offered to help. Their offer was rejected. They took offence, and wrote to King Ahasuerus, getting it stopped (4:1–6).

From then on, relationships with the Jews were broken off. Later, the Samaritans, claiming to be followers of Moses, built their own temple on Mount Gerizim (John 4:19–24). The Gospels vividly portray the hostility of the two peoples.

Ezra chapter 5 describes how Haggai and Zechariah stirred up Zerubbabel to take up the work again. This time it was a Persian governor who questioned the building, and wrote about it to the new king, Darius I. Darius dug up the records and, finding that Cyrus had authorized it, allowed it to continue. The work was completed in his reign (6:14–22).

The returned exiles had insisted on rigorous segregation from the surrounding people. This was something they had learnt from Ezekiel. After the Second World War a similar situation arose, when Orthodox Jews, from Hitler's death camps, came to the United States. There, liberal American Jews had long ago given up strict observance of the Law. The immigrants took over control of the Rabbinical schools, imposing their fundamentalism, with the moral authority that suffering for their faith had given them.

The story of Nehemiah fits in very convincingly at this point. He arrived seventy years later, when zeal had given way to disillusion and apathy. While a general hostility continued between Jews and their neighbours, intermarriage had nevertheless become commonplace. Nehemiah had tried to deal with it and failed. He had restored the city walls. Another man, a priest, was needed to restore the Law.

Ezra's personal story begins in Ezra 7. He left Babylon with a company of Levites and with gifts of gold and silver, the amount being considerably exaggerated (7:16). The gifts were given by the Persian king and his counsellors to pay for temple sacrifices, to appease God's wrath against the Persian royal house. Ezra was given privileges for the Levites, who were to be exempt from tax. He was also empowered to appoint magistrates and judges, who could impose the death penalty for breaches of the Law. Here is an example of a state 'church', a theocracy, imposed with a vengeance by a normally tolerant non-Jewish empire! Ezra was delighted with the arrangement, and thanked God for it.

Unlike Nehemiah, Ezra refused the offer of a royal escort. He had told the king that God would protect them. Instead, he and his followers prepared for the journey with prayer and fasting (8:21–23). It was indeed a journey of faith, as the wilderness was infested by robbers, and Ezra's party was transporting a considerable treasure. Ezra was concerned for the safe delivery of every article, down to the smallest spoon. God did protect them, and they arrived safely, the treasure intact.

Ezra was immediately confronted by the problem of intermarriage (chapter 9). He was told that even the priests and Levites were involved (compare Nehemiah 13:28). Ezra was horrified. He wept and prayed, and tore his robes and hair. The exile, he believed, had been caused by this wickedness. Now, with a restored nation and a rebuilt temple, was it to start all over again?

The people started to weep with him (10:1). They too began to confess their sins. A great revival in East Africa began when a church council was called to discuss divisions and other evils, and the Holy Spirit swept the bishops to their knees, confessing their own sins and asking for forgiveness. Seeing the broken hearts of their leaders, the hardness of the people's hearts was also melted. Tears of penitence move more hearts than rebuke. Do we need to pray for the humbling gift of tears?

All agreed that the covenant should be renewed. While Ezra fasted the whole people was summoned. Within three days a crowd assembled, and Ezra began to speak to them. Then it started to pour with rain (chapter 10). As the matter was too big to be settled quickly, action was delayed, but the separation of intermarried couples did take place, no doubt causing much heartbreak.

The story of Ezra continues in Nehemiah 8. This describes how Ezra stood on a pulpit and read to the people the Book of the Law. He not only read it, he explained it (8:8). In most churches today, sermons which teach and explain the Bible text are out of fashion. In how many churches do people come bringing their Bible with them, expecting such instruction? This, no doubt, is the reason why the Bible and the doctrines of the Church are so little understood by those who hear them declaimed Sunday by Sunday.

After this mammoth teaching session, the people's sorrow was turned into joy. Verse 10 contains one of the golden verses celebrated in song. Everyone went home to celebrate the feast of Tabernacles, building booths, as many Jews in Palestine do today. There had been nothing like it, adds the Chronicler, since the days of Joshua.

All this took place in the seventh month, in which, according to the

Law (Leviticus 16:29), the Day of Atonement was to be annually celebrated. Ezra's work came to a climax with a day of national repentance and confession, ending in a solemn renewal of the covenant (Nehemiah 9). It was signed, in the people's name, by princes, priests and Levites (verse 38). Their names are listed in chapter 10. This resulted in the decision to renew much that had been long neglected, the keeping of the sabbath, the year of Jubilee, the tithe, and other offerings. It was also decided that every family should cast lots to ensure that one in ten of their number should live in Jerusalem, together with the rulers of the city. The others should live in the villages outside. Beyond the city walls stretched another wall, both higher and stronger: the wall of the Law. It separated Jew from Gentile with far greater effect. Ezra had done his work well. Nehemiah's walls were knocked down. Ezra's wall still stands today.

The Books of Chronicles

Before leaving the work of the Chronicler, some mention should be made of his two earlier books, the special concerns and the theme that links all four books together.

The Chronicler was a priest, and his main concern was with the temple, its building, priests, rituals, sacrifices and music. Ezekiel's vision of the restored temple and its purity has influenced all his thinking.

The first 9 chapters show his concern for genealogy. If the Jew is to be separate from all other races, it is important to know who is a Jew. To be acceptable you had to be able to trace your descent back to Abraham, who was a descendant of Shem. Those who were descended from Noah's other sons were not members of the chosen race. In view of Ezekiel's teaching about the purity of priests and Levites, their ancestry too was important (1 Chronicles 24). The rights of those with special duties had also to be protected (chapters 25–27).

The Chronicler's story begins with Saul's death and the crowning of David. David's first task is to take Jerusalem (chapter 11) and bring into it the ark of God (13:15–16). His next concern is to build God's house (chapter 17). David's sin with Bathsheba is omitted. It is irrelevant to the author's theme. But his sin of numbering the tribes is included, as this led to his purchase of the altar site. The rest of the book deals with the preparations David made for the temple building. It includes the glorious ascription of praise used in the offertory prayer of the Communion Service (29:11).

The first seven chapters of 2 Chronicles is taken up with the building and dedication of the temple by Solomon. The rest of the book, mainly copied from 2 Kings, shows how idolatry led to the exile and the destruction of the temple. This leads naturally into the Book of Ezra with its description of the return of priests, Levites and temple treasure, the rebuilding of the temple by Zerubbabel, the teaching and enforcing of the Law by Ezra, and to the climax of the story, the renewal of the covenant. Typically, the names of all who signed it are listed (Nehemiah 10).

The story of Nehemiah is fitted into this. The building of the walls are important only because they protect the purity of the temple and its worshippers by shutting out the Gentiles. Historically, Nehemiah's presence at the reading of the Law (Nehemiah 8:9) is very doubtful, but, seen from the Chronicler's point of view, Nehemiah was certainly there, in spirit at least. The work of the two men dovetailed, but it is the priest and the temple that are of paramount importance.

In Israel today there is an unresolved tension between the government of what is still technically a secular state, and the Orthodox party wanting a theocracy. Both have need of each other, but their interests conflict. The government is concerned with the walls of political security. The Orthodox party is concerned to enforce the Law. A similar state of conflict and interdependent need is to be found in the history of Church and state in Britain.

The Book of Joel

Joel (about 400BC) was driven to prophesy by a devastating plague of locusts. He likens it to an advancing army, with graphic detail which describes the awful suffering of man and beast.

For Joel, the worst result was that the temple sacrifices had to stop, through lack of provision. It is an outlook typical of the Chronicler and Ezra. Joel sees the plague as a judgment for sin, and calls the priest to proclaim a national day of fasting and prayer (Joel 1:14; 2:15). He has, however, been influenced by the earlier prophets. Ritual acts of repentance are not enough. There must be sorrow of heart, and earnest prayer (2:13, 17). Then, he believes, God will drive the locusts away, and restore prosperity (2:18–27).

How do we interpret natural disaster? Sometimes its connection with sin is clear. Wars in Africa have prevented international agencies from spraying locust concentrations before their devastating swarms which disregard national boundaries. The firing of the Kuwait oil fields and the pollution of the Gulf will bring all kinds of disaster, but not, however, exclusively to those most responsible.

Other disasters, such as earthquakes and volcanic eruption, have no such obvious connection. They remind us that we are not in full control of our environment. We have no security other than God. Our idols are shaken, our values reassessed. Disaster calls out the worst and the best in us. It is a revealing test of who we are. It is a day of judgment.

To Joel, the disaster of locusts foreshadowed such a judgment day. Of this he has two visions, both of them important for us today.

The first is the outpouring of the Spirit on all flesh. His words were quoted by Peter on the day of Pentecost (Joel 2:28–32; Acts 2:16–21). Throughout the Old Testament we read of the Spirit being outpoured on special people, at special times, for a special purpose.

John the Baptist was told that he would recognize Jesus when he saw the Spirit coming upon him and remaining. All Jesus' words and actions flowed at all times from the Spirit. This Spirit was poured out at Pentecost, and is given to all believers. Sadly, we have so often failed to possess our promised possessions. Today there is a new fulfilment of Joel's prophecy, as the Spirit sweeps, with Pentecostal power, through churches of every denomination and race.

Joel's second vision is of God challenging the surrounding nations to unite, and wage war on the holy city. Then, God will judge them with a decisive defeat. They will be destroyed. Jerusalem will be protected, blessed and established for ever.

On the surface this is a very narrow and nationalistic vision, typical of the outlook of the Chronicler and Ezra. It is a far cry from the vision of all three Isaiahs. But, like all prophets, Joel spoke truer than he knew. His vision bears a strong resemblance to that of John's Book of Revelation, with its description of the final reaping (Revelation 14:14–20) and the final battle of Armageddon (Revelation 16:15–21).

These biblical visions, ridiculed in the past by liberal theologians and secular humanists, are today taking on a terrible reality. The war with Kuwait was swift. Only one army was destroyed, but it was enough to darken sun, moon and stars with a pall of smoke. Armageddon, or Meggido, is the strategic pass where the main road north and south is met by the road from the east. If the state of Israel lives under threat from Arab neighbours, the new Israel, the Church, lives under threat of a rising tide of naked evil, violence and persecution, on a scale that is new. Her defence lies not with tanks or Trident missiles, but with the Spirit of the Lord, (Isaiah 63:11) and the Word of God, *Christus Victor* (Revelation 19:11–16). A nuclear war, destroying the earth by fire, can now be envisaged (2 Peter 3:12). The new heaven and the new earth is beyond our imagination. It can be pictured only in symbols.

The future kingdom   *Zechariah 9–14*

The last six chapters of Zechariah were written about 338BC, about sixty years after Joel. The conquering invaders are the Greeks. The reference of Zechariah 9:13 is probably to the army of Alexander the Great who, in

333BC, overran Syria, Tyre and Sidon and what is now the Gaza strip.

Jeremiah had warned that Judah would again be overrun, but he believed that Jerusalem would be saved by the coming of the Messiah. Jerusalem fell to the Greeks, and the coming of the Messiah was delayed for another three centuries. Then Jesus deliberately fulfilled the prophecy of Zechariah 9:9–10, by riding into Jerusalem on a donkey. What a wonderful call to a threatened people is found in verse 12. The Lord is their shepherd. He will save his flock, precious to him like jewels in his crown.

In chapter 10 we read of God's anger with false shepherds, the priests and the Levites of the day. People are called to pray for the latter rain, which has been interpreted by Christians as the fresh outpouring of God's Spirit which has been experienced by the Church through the ages in times of renewal and revival. The 'early rain' softened the ground for the planting of the seed. The 'latter rain' was vital for a good harvest. God will raise up new leaders—'cornerstone' and 'tent peg'. These titles point back to Isaiah 28:16 and Isaiah 22:20–25. They were fulfilled by Christ. He was the cornerstone (Luke 20:17–18; compare 1 Peter 2:6–8). He was the nail on which was hung the burden of his Father's house. He was cut down, and the burden of our sin fell away.

The prophecy of 10:8–12 is of great importance today. It continues a promise that all the scattered Jews would return home. Only the remnant from Babylon had returned. Those scattered in northern lands by Assyria, and those who had fled to Egypt, had not returned. Nor did they. The scattering, or dispersion, went on. After the destruction of Jerusalem in AD70, it gathered momentum, until Jews were to be found in nations all over the world.

After the murder of six million Jews by Hitler, the pressure for a mass return to Palestine began. Now it has become a flood, and Jews are rejoicing that this prophecy is now being fulfilled.

But what about the Palestinians, so forcibly displaced? These verses may point to a Jewish return, but make no mention of another conquest driving out the resident tribes and setting up another national state. There remains Jesus' parable of the vineyard, with its warning of Jewish dispossession.

How does the Church, as the new Israel, relate to Judaism today? The problem was thrashed out by St Paul in Romans 9–11. He saw them as a branch of the vine cut off, but able to be grafted in again. This was his yearning for his own people.

There is now a growing number of Jews who accept Jesus as Israel's Messiah. His kingdom claims no earthly territory. The ingathering of his people, both Jew and Gentile, need displace no one. Where there is justice and peace, the wall of partition has been broken down, land can be shared.

Chapter 11 (continued in 13:7–9) is about bad shepherds. The three got rid of were three high priests who were deposed. But who is the speaker, holding the two staves Beauty and Bands?—in the RSV they are translated Grace and Union. Some say they represent the temple sacrifices and the Law. The Bishop of Chichester, in an article on the work of a bishop, writes of Beauty as his responsibility for worship, and Bands, discipline for maintaining the unity of the Church.

The shepherd loses patience, and resigns. He snaps the two staves as a sign of breaking his covenant with the people, and destroying their unity (compare Ezekiel 37:19). Contemptuously, they reward his services with the price of a slave, which he flings down on the temple floor. Whatever may have been the original situation for this mysterious passage, St Matthew (27:9) sees it as a prophecy of the price of Jesus' betrayal, though he mistakes the source of his quotation!

Malachi had complained how little God's people valued all he had done for them. Jesus' death did destroy the old covenant, and brought division to the nation, as he said it would (Luke 12:51–53). That these verses were also in Jesus' mind is clear from the quotations of Zechariah 13:7 (Matthew 26:31), as also, perhaps, verse 6.

The last three chapters bring visions of the day of the Lord to be fulfilled in history and at the end of time. They are relevant today. Certainly Jerusalem is a cup of trembling, and a burdensome stone to her neighbours!

Out of the confusion three clear predictions shine through. Jerusalem will be attacked by the Gentiles, and fall amidst great suffering. The nations that attack her will be destroyed. The Lord will one day stand on the Mount of Olives, and reign over all the earth. Wishful thinking? These prophecies, which echo those of Jeremiah and Ezekiel, were fulfilled. Greeks and Romans both destroyed the city. Both Empires were themselves destroyed. Jesus stood on the Mount of Olives. He reigns over peoples in all the earth. We believe he will come again and finally establish his kingdom.

The imagery of these chapters is picked up in John's Revelation. The cleansing fountain, like Ezekiel's river, is also described (Zechariah 13; Revelation 21:6). More important, Jesus claimed to be its source (John 4:14). For Christians it is the cleansing fountain of his blood. Another verse that points us to him is Zechariah 12:10.

The book ends with a vision of Jerusalem as a centre of worship for all nations. All that defiles has been refined by fire (13:9). Even the pots and pans, like the bells on the horses' necks, are holy to the Lord. Distinctions of sacred and secular are abolished. Everything exists for God's glory (14:16–21).

Alas, we come down to earth with a bump. The feast of Tabernacles must be forcibly imposed, and the Canaanite—the Palestinian—is still excluded.

For further reading

Psalm 119:105–112; Romans 9:10–11; 1 Corinthians 7:12–16; 2 Corinthians 6:14–18

For group discussion

1. What is your attitude towards 'Keeping Sunday Special'?

2. How do you regard intermarriage with Christians of other denominations, and with people of other religions or none?

3. Should particular biblical prophecies be used to justify present-day actions?

For private reflection

1. What can you learn from Nehemiah's prayer life?

2. What discouragements do you face as a Christian? How do you handle them?

3. Does mixing in society tarnish us?

15

Stories of Protest, Songs and Sayings

Ruth; Jonah; Lamentations; Psalms; Proverbs

We now come to the books of the Old Testament known to the Jews as the Writings. They lacked the authority of the Law and the Prophets, and some only narrowly gained admittance to the canon, that is the list of books accepted as Holy Scripture.

In 331BC the Greeks conquered the Persian Empire and the Greek language became universal. The Hebrew Bible was translated into Greek and was known as the Septuagint. St Paul's quotations are often taken from this version.

More books were added by Jews outside Jerusalem, who lived in Alexandria, a strong centre of Judaism (Acts 18:24). In AD90 the canon of the Old Testament was closed. Some of the books that failed that particular test are to be found amongst the apocryphal (literally, 'hidden') books such as Ecclesiasticus, the Books of Maccabees and the Book of Wisdom. These books, which were included among the Old Testament Books by the Roman Catholic Church, and so are found in the Jerusalem Bible, are now being included in the new Bibles such as the New Revised Standard Version and the Revised English Bible. They help to bridge the gap between the Old and the New Testaments, and we will be referring especially to the Books of Maccabees. We will, however, be studying only the canonical Writings.

The Writings vary greatly. They consist of history, stories, songs, wise sayings, a love poem and a drama. Their dates also vary. While some of the Psalms and Proverbs, for instance, may go back to the time of Solomon, most of the books were written about 200BC.

Two stories of protest   *Ruth; Jonah*

Ezra had slammed and barred the doors and gates of the temple and the city against the Gentiles. The Gentiles were considered to be a danger to the purity of the Jewish race and religion. So, out with them! But what of the vision of all three Isaiahs? They had seen Israel's vocation as a light shining in a dark world, bringing God's salvation to all peoples. You can't both preach salvation and exclude people, though many Christians have tried to do just that!

Protest against Ezra's policy of exclusion was expressed in two very different stories—Ruth and Jonah.

The Book of Ruth

As mentioned at the beginning of Chapter 6, Ruth was the great-grandmother of David. Now is the time to go back to re-read her story, and remember what you thought it was about.

It begins in Bethlehem. The name means 'House of Bread', but when the story begins, the bread had run out. There was a famine. Naomi, her husband and two sons migrated, as so many hungry people are doing today. They settled in Moab, a long-standing enemy, with whom they had fought many wars, and who enslaved them for eighteen years (Judges 3:14–21).

Naomi's sons, being separated from their own people, took Moabite wives. They would have probably been worshippers of Chemosh, referred to in 1 Kings 11:7 as 'the abomination of Moab'. It seems, however, that they adopted the religion of their husbands.

Then tragedy struck. Both the father and the two sons died. Maybe it was cholera or some other killer disease, or an accident. Naomi must have asked, 'Why?' No doubt Ezra, and the first readers of this story, could have told her. It was God's punishment for putting food before faith, deserting the Promised Land and marrying her sons to idol worshippers.

Yet what joy Naomi must have had teaching them her faith. Now, in deepest sorrow, she sets off to return home to Bethlehem. She tells her daughters-in-law to leave her and return to their own people and gods. One of them does so. Not Ruth. In unforgettable words she declares her loyalty to Naomi, Naomi's people and Naomi's God. They return to Bethlehem together. Significantly, they arrive at the time of the barley harvest.

The story goes on to tell how loyally and lovingly Ruth served her mother-in-law, and how she gleaned in the fields of Boaz, who proved to be her husband's kinsman. Coached by Naomi, she asks him, through a silent action, to take her as his wife and, as the law required, raise up for the dead a son to inherit his land. This Boaz was glad to do, though first he had to clear the situation with a kinsman with a prior claim. The story ends with the birth of Obed, the father of Jesse, the father of David.

This is not just a story about loyalty, though it is that. It is primarily about the attitude of Jews towards foreigners who came to share their faith. Note how often Ruth is referred to as 'Ruth the Moabitess', and how highly she is praised.

Nehemiah had cursed Jews who had married Samaritans, and Ezra had forced them to separate from their wives. We have seen how priests, prophets and the scribes who wrote the books of Scripture had nearly all been consistently hostile to any mingling of the races. They had good reason, for the dangers had been only too apparent.

The original promise to Abraham, however, still stood. Through him and his descendants God's blessing was to be given to all nations. This was the vision of the Book of Isaiah. The Gentiles would flock to the holy city, and the temple would be a house of prayer for all nations.

If Ruth, the Moabitess, was good enough to be accepted as the great-grandmother of King David, who could criticize such an intermarriage? That is the point of the story. Gentile believers are to be accepted on equal terms. The coming of Jesus made it crucial. It was mainly because the Jews refused to accept the Gentiles that they also refused to accept the gospel.

The Book of Jonah

Nothing could be more different from the quiet pastoral tale of the lovely Ruth than Jonah. It is a stormy surrealist story of a cantankerous prophet, told with the biting wit and punch of *Private Eye!*

The only thing most people know about Jonah is that he was swallowed by a whale. People have wasted time and effort trying to prove that survival after such an experience is possible. In doing so they miss both the humour and the point of the story. It should have started with 'Once upon a time...'

There had actually been a prophet called Jonah (2 Kings 14:25). The writer chose to attach this story to his name. It has meaning for us as we identify ourselves with him.

God called Jonah to do a job for him. Jonah didn't want to do it, so he ran away. The people of Nineveh, Assyrians, were not just pagans. They were the cruelest and most wicked people Jonah had ever come across. He wanted nothing to do with them. Hitler and his Nazis couldn't have been worse.

He ran as far as the sea, and then got on a boat bound for the end of the world. Tarshish is in Spain. It must have cost him a pretty penny, and not just in money. Jews hated and feared the sea.

But you can't run away from God (Psalm 139:9–10), an awesome or comforting thought according to your relationship with him. The ship's progress is stopped by a storm. The sailors, horrid pagans, pray. Jonah, the pious Jew, sleeps. Running away from God is an emotionally exhausting business. They wake him and tell him to pray too. His God is the God who made the sea. Jonah has the honesty to confess that it is his sin that has got them all into this trouble. He tells them to throw him overboard and then they'll be safe. Note the irony—Ezra's policy is reversed. The pagans, forced to eject the Jew, do their best to save him! The storm gets worse. Reluctantly they abandon him.

'And the Lord appointed a great fish to swallow up Jonah.' Those three days and nights were quoted by Jesus as typifying his experience of death (Matthew 12:40). Dead to the world but safe, Jonah had time to repent and pray. It was lucky for him he had been trained as a child to learn Psalms by heart. He hadn't got his Bible with him. What a comfort they were to him now. The snatches of quotations come from different Psalms (for example, 42:7).

What sort of whale swallows us when we say 'No' to God? It is a kind of dying. Despair at first perhaps, then rage, self-justification, lies and self-pity. Hopefully we come through to confession, repentance, and an experience of salvation and resurrection.

Jonah is resurrected. The challenge he stalled at again confronts him. He obeys, goes to Nineveh and preaches. The people, from the king downward, all repent. Even the animals join in fasting. Jonah's mission is a brilliant success, and Jonah is disgusted.

Only now is the real reason for his disobedience made plain. He knew God wanted to save the people of Nineveh, and he, Jonah, didn't want them saved. It wasn't fair of God. 'Wicked people ought to be punished.' Is that why many church people react to Aids sufferers with so little compassion?

Jonah is angry. He sulks like a child, and says he wants to die. 'Do you do well to be angry?' asks God. No answer. Jonah goes and camps elsewhere. A gourd magically grows up to shadow him from the sun. Jonah enjoys it. In the morning a worm destroys it. Pure Disney cartoon stuff. Up comes the sun, wham blows the hot wind. Jonah, fainting, again wants to die.

Then God asks once more, 'Do you do well to be angry?' 'Yes' answers Jonah, now quite furious. Then comes the punchline. 'You pity a gourd you neither planted nor made to grow. Should not I pity Nineveh, people so ignorant of me and my ways that they can't tell their right hand from their left, good from evil?' A nice postscript includes the cattle, also in God's care.

The teaching of this story would be so shocking to Jews of Ezra's day, it had to be told in this way, with wit, and fairy-tale exaggeration, to make them laugh. But the message was serious and profound, its challenge revolutionary.

The story leaves us wondering if we really want everyone to be converted, and joining our church. African and Asian immigrants, drug addicts, homosexuals with Aids, would we give them a welcome? Already they have experienced so much rejection. If they flooded in and began to outnumber us, would we walk out, applauding Isaiah perhaps with our hands, but voting for Ezra with our feet? The matter is crucial. It led Jesus to the cross (Matthew 21:43–44). It was for this reason that Jewish mobs howled for Paul's death too (Acts 22:21–22).

The Book of Lamentations

This book contains five psalms mourning the destruction of Jerusalem. Originally they were thought to be the work of Jeremiah, but they are very different and are probably by different writers.

They gave the exiles words with which to express their grief. Also, by recognizing God's hand in the event, they gave the people hope. The teaching of Ezekiel was not enough. They needed songs, as we need hymns, to bring the teaching home to the heart.

Song 1 (chapter 1) emphasizes that the fall of Jerusalem was due to sin. Verse 12 has been made famous by Stainer's *Crucifixion* which applies to Jesus.

Song 2 (chapter 2) sees the fall of the city not as the work of the enemy, but of God, who swallowed the city as the whale swallowed Jonah. The exile was a national death, preparing the Jews for a new resurrected life. Verse 15 also leads us to the crucifixion scene.

Song 3 (chapter 3) is a cry of personal anguish. It leads us to a cry of hope. If stoicism or false piety makes us stifle the first, we cannot release the second. Our hope is in a God of compassion. It is the cross that gives us such assurance. Verse 23 inspired the great hymn. Again the theme of waiting appears. Acceptance is part of hope, not its opposite. Verse 30 also reminds us of Jesus at his trial. God does not want to afflict. He wants us to repent and turn to him. If he seems to have hidden himself, and be deaf to our entreaties, it is because he wants us to persevere. What depth is discovered here.

Song 4 (chapter 4) describes the awfulness of the siege and exile. It ends with a warning to Edom.

Song 5 (chapter 5) is a prayer for restoration and renewal. Note that verse 7 voices the proverb which Ezekiel countered.

Songs for all seasons   *The Psalms*

The Jews were famous for their songs, as Psalm 137 indicates. Just as all the Law was attributed to Moses, so all Psalms were to David, the 'sweet psalmist of Israel' (2 Samuel 23:1). The title 'of David' affixed to so many refers, however, to the name of a collection, as does 'of Asaph' (Psalms 73–83) and 'of Korah' (Psalms 84–85). Our Book of Psalms is a collection taken from several collections. It is arranged in five books, each ending in a shout of praise, 'Blessed be God' (Psalm 41:13; 72:18–19; 89:52; 106:48; 150:6).

Jewish poetry did not rhyme, but was rhythmic. Verses had two clauses linked in pairs by a completing or contrasting idea. So they can be said or sung antiphonally, that is by alternate voices or choirs. In some, each verse begins with consecutive letters of the alphabet. An example of this is Psalm 119, in which each verse of each stanza begins with consecutive letters of the Hebrew alphabet, which helps to explain its length!

The Psalms were used in temple worship. Some, like the 'Songs of Ascents' (Psalms 120–134) were linked to a particular festival, in this case, a pilgrimage. Today, Psalm 122 is usually recited by Christian pilgrims when they first come within sight of holy city of Jerusalem. The last Psalm of the group was sung on arrival at the temple, and calls upon the priests, and all who serve there, to join the pilgrims in blessing the Lord. Psalm 122 is also a nice Psalm to sing on the way to church. Psalm 134 is part of the Church's night prayers, sometimes called Compline.

The Psalms were accompanied by a large number of instruments, and sometimes dancing (Psalm 150). Hands were lifted up, and there was clapping. This richness, natural to African and Caribbean churches, is now, through renewal, entering some of the more sober churches of the West, bringing rejoicing to some and alarm to others.

The Psalms were Jesus' hymnbook. He would have sung them at home with his family and at the synagogue every sabbath. As a child he would have learnt a large number, if not all of them, by heart. He quoted them in his teaching, nourished his life and strengthened his faith on them. Try praying some of them with him.

Take for instance Psalm 40. As you read verses 1–8 you can identify yourself with him as he emerges from the wilderness after his struggle in the miry pit of temptation stirred up by the devil, a struggle which ended in victory and the comforting ministry of angels. He is consecrating himself to a life of sacrificial obedience and love. See, in the remaining verses, his ministry of teaching. The iniquities of verse 12 are ours. He identifies himself with them (2 Corinthians 5:21). He chose to share the weakness of our humanity and, like us, was totally dependent on his Father.

Go on to read Psalm 118, this time identifying with Jesus as he rides into Jerusalem on Palm Sunday. Join in his praise and trust in God his

Father and Lord who will enable him to overcome rather than destroy his enemies, and preserve his life. Jesus would already have been given the assurance of hope in the resurrection in Psalm 16:8–11. All this experience is for us too. Recognize the verse (22) about the stone, which he later quoted. Identify with the crowd hailing him in verses 25–26. The Jewish word *Hosannah* is the imperative form of the verb to save, and comes from the same root as that of the name Jesus. 'Save now', we cry with them. Then read with awe, and accept with thanksgiving, the final verses expressing his willing self-sacrifice for our salvation. He is the lamb which God provided (Genesis 22:8).

Jesus sang a Psalm with his disciples just before leaving for the Garden of Gethsemane. He was praying Psalm 22 on the cross. Note how triumphantly it ends. He died with verse 5 of Psalm 31 on his lips. It was a verse that Mary would have taught him to pray, as every Jewish mother taught her children, last thing at night before falling asleep. Now it is part of Compline, the Church's night prayers.

Some other Psalms, or rather some verses of Psalms, have been taken as relating to Christ. Psalms 47 and 68 point to his ascension, as St Paul recognized (Ephesians 4:8). St John linked Psalm 69:9 with Jesus cleansing the temple (John 2:17). Much of the royal Psalms (Psalms 20; 21; 24; 45) can be applied to him. More importantly, Jesus himself interpreted the Psalms in this way, as he quoted Psalm 110:1 (Matthew 22:41–46).

The Church has always treasured the Psalms as a storehouse of public and private devotion. Their recital in the monastic offices of daily prayer—Anglican matins and evensong—still goes on. Paraphrased as hymns they are cherished and sung by the Church of Scotland. They are indeed songs for all seasons.

There are Psalms suitable for night (Psalm 4) and morning (Psalm 5), for going on a journey (Psalm 121), for harvest (Psalm 65), for times of sickness (Psalm 6) and approaching death (Psalms 23 and 39). They express sorrow for sin (Psalms 51; 130), thanksgiving for forgiveness (Psalm 32) and every kind of blessing (Psalm 13), our longing for God (Psalms 27; 42; 63) as well as our security in his knowledge of us (Psalm 139). Notice how the Psalms that cry out in trouble for God's help end in praise and confident thanksgiving, before help comes (Psalms 13; 28).

Psalm 19 and the long Psalm 119 express the Psalmist's love of God's Law. We are apt to react negatively to the idea of law. The Ten Commandments are now very rarely recited in church. We take our attitude to the Law from the criticisms of Jesus against its abuse, and from St Paul's resistance to its claims to be accepted as essential to the salvation of the Gentiles. It is seen as a burden too great to be borne. But this is due to all the detailed regulations loaded on it, to define its application. Seen in its original Mosaic simplicity it was an object of love, then and through the centuries. Jews have been, and are, willing to die for it. As we read the Law as expounded by Jesus in the Sermon on the Mount, do we have a similar love for it? As we turn our hearts towards obedience to Christ, our Way, we can meditate on the wonderful words of Psalm 119:25–40, and make them our own.

Many of the Psalms are Psalms of praise and thanksgiving and some of these are grouped together (Psalms 95–101; 145–150). Some praise God, for his creation (Psalms 8; 65; 147; 148), some for his saving acts in history (Psalms 105; 106). It would be a good exercise to write a psalm of thanksgiving for our own personal history, or that of our church or nation.

Dip, explore, browse and pray these Psalms. Their richness is inexhaustible. It is good to learn some favourites by heart. You might need them when, like Jonah, you find yourself caught in trouble without a Bible to hand. Meditation on them can be a form of stocking Mother Hubbard's cupboard, so that, when need arises, it isn't bare. God's Spirit is able to select just the right verse to give you the help you need, and bring it into your mind.

Two problems, however, usually arise for those who set about this. One concerns the anger expressed, and the curses the Psalmist calls down on his enemies, for example, in Psalm 109. It is important to understand the content of such Psalms. Christians in Britain are secure, but many of the Psalms were written at the time of the Greek King Antiochus Epiphanes. In 167BC he desecrated the Jewish temple by setting up a pagan altar to Zeus on its site. He publicly burnt the scrolls of the Law, forbade circumcision and the keeping of the sabbath, and did all he could to stamp out the Jewish religion. The horrific story of cruelty and martyrdom is described in the Books of the Maccabees (for example, 2 Maccabees 6–7), and is reflected in Psalms 74, 79 and 102. More than one and a half centuries later Jesus was to teach and demonstrate love and forgiveness for his enemies. It was a revolutionary teaching which, even today, Christians find hard to accept.

What are we to make of such Psalms today, as we meet them in private prayer? They are usually excluded from public worship. A traditional answer has been to spiritualize the enemies, taking them to be the forces of evil around us, and within (Ephesians 6:12). A more modern answer is to see them as giving an example of honesty in expressing our negative emotions to God. Prayer isn't offering to God sentiments we consider suitable. God isn't taken in, and knows the unsuitable ones we conceal, even from ourselves. Prayer is opening up the whole of ourselves to God, warts and all, a true encounter of our raw reality and God, who is the supreme and ultimate reality. He meets us in the here and now of our truth. Though we may repress it, we do hate, and we do get angry, even with God. He knows it, even if we don't.

'Vent your anger upon the Almighty' was the advice of a wise spiritual director. Only with him is it safe. Kept inside us it corrodes. Loosed on others it hurts and destroys. Offered to God it is cleansed and healed.

The second problem is that of the self-righteousness expressed in so many Psalms. Psalm 18:20–24 to us sounds smug. The Jews believed that God saved and protected only the righteous, and for them, the righteous were those who obeyed God's Law. Under the cruel domination of Antiochus, the Jews were sacrificing their lives for their obedience, which, as we see in Psalm 119, sprang from love. They couldn't understand why God seemed to be abandoning them. They cried out their pain and bewilderment, but hung on to their faith.

As we meditate on these Psalms we could ask ourselves if we would be prepared to pay such a price for our obedience. Perhaps it is we who are smug!

A book of practical ethics   *Proverbs*

With the Book of Proverbs we come down to earth with a bump. The passionate outpourings of the Psalms are replaced by the practical, cautious, even calculating morality of practical wisdom.

Wise men and wise women (2 Samuel 14:2) formed a recognized group of people. They were less highly regarded than priests and prophets, and may have first been gathered together at the court of Solomon. As we have seen, Solomon was himself credited with composing three thousand proverbs (1 Kings 4:32).

Like the Psalms, these were collections of such sayings, which were attributed to Solomon as the Psalms were to David. This book is a collection, ancient and modern, covering different periods. Those in chapters 10–29 are earlier, and some may even be Solomon's. If so, it is a pity that Rehoboam didn't take his father's advice given in Proverbs 15:1 and 16:18. It might have saved the kingdom from being split. Perhaps Solomon should have taken his own advice about training a child (Proverbs 22:6). They might also give a surprising inside view of the problems Solomon may have had with his wives! (See Proverbs 21:9.)

The book starts with a group of proverbs in praise of Wisdom (Proverbs 1:20–23; 3:13–20; 4:5–13; 8–9). It ends with the famous alphabetic poem on the virtuous wife (Proverbs 31:10–31). How relevant is she today?

Her object is not self-fulfilment but self-giving, which springs from faith in God. Her sphere of service starts with her family, but extends to her needy neighbours. She is hard-working, yet she keeps a kindly tongue. Her husband can trust her. Her employment enhances, rather than diminishes his reputation and sense of self-worth. Her reward is to be honoured and loved.

Women in the Bible hold an honoured position. Even alien women like Rahab, a prostitute, and Jael, slayer of Sisera, are respected. Miriam, Moses' sister, and Deborah, the prophetess and judge, are accepted as national leaders. Rebekah, Abigail, and the great woman of Shunem were well able to take the initiative and play leading roles. Sarah could even lead Abraham astray, but she never questioned his authority to make the final decision. She is quoted as a model for Christian wives (1 Peter 3:6).

Proverbs is a book to be dipped into rather than read through, and it comes across with particular clarity in the Good News Bible. Like *Hamlet*, it is full of quotations. To mention one, just to whet the appetite, the proverb found in 25:21 was quoted by Jesus in the Sermon on the Mount (Matthew 5:43–45). It is the nearest the Old Testament gets to his teaching about forgiveness. But we all know the difference between coals of fire, experienced as shame, and the healing oil of true forgiving love.

Proverbs assumes that right behaviour reaps earthly rewards. The gospel of success is today preached by some American 'televangelists'. As with all false gospels, it contains a grain of truth. In a small settled society, good men and women are honoured, and honest workers get the jobs. The fostering of good relationships in industry is a managerial skill. Strikes mean losses. But, in many businesses today, those who refuse to cooperate in shady deals forfeit promotion, and many even lose their jobs. Immoral practices may eventually be shown up. When they are, resulting ruin usually hits the innocent.

The inclusion of this book in the canon of Scripture shows that God doesn't just speak through prophets and visions. He gave us reason and common sense, and expects us to use them. Wisdom, the fruit of observation, thought and experience, is a gift of God. Note the emphatic repetition that it begins with the fear, that is the reverent acknowledgment, of God, influencing our thoughts and attitudes at every level. The fool spoken of here is not an idiot. He or she is the person who rejects belief in God (Psalm 14:1).

In the early chapters, Wisdom is exalted to such a high degree as to be God-like. In the Book of Wisdom, found in the Apocrypha, Wisdom is referred to as 'a breath of the power of God ... a reflection of the eternal light, untarnished mirror of God's active power, image of his goodness' (Wisdom 7:25–26 JB). This for us has overtones relating Wisdom both to the Holy Spirit and to Jesus, the breath and image of God. As usual, the Greeks had a word for it, not *Sophia*, their usual word for wisdom, but

Logos, which means 'Word'. This is the word—'Word'—used to translate 'Wisdom' in the Greek translation of the Hebrew Bible, and is the word John uses to describe the cosmic Christ (John 1:1–3; compare Proverbs 8:22–27). Paul calls Christ 'the wisdom of God' (1 Corinthians 1:24).

It is interesting to note that Wisdom is portrayed in Proverbs, and the Book of Wisdom, as feminine. It reminds us that both male and female qualities are to be found in God, a truth the Church today is rediscovering.

For further reading

Acts 13:38–52; 22:1–23; Ephesians 2:11–22; 1 Peter 3:1–9

For group discussion

1. What sort of welcome would your church give to: outsiders coming from other places or other churches? New converts? Enquirers from marginalized groups like addicts or Aids sufferers?

2. What place do the Psalms have in your worship? How can they best be used?

3. Has the virtuous wife of Proverbs 31 anything relevant to say to us?

For private reflection

1. What sort of welcome do strangers get coming to your church? What more could be done to welcome them?

2. What does Jonah's whale signify to you?

3. How can the Psalms help you in your private prayers?

16

The Problem of Pain and Suffering

Ecclesiastes; Job; Song of Solomon; Esther; Daniel

A dirge of disillusionment   *Ecclesiastes*

This book very nearly didn't get accepted as Scripture. But how wonderful that it did. The Scriptures contain something for everyone, even the disillusioned. Ecclesiastes rejects the idea that goodness is rewarded in this life, and, as it foresees no other, that is cause enough for being disillusioned. Paul would have understood this (1 Corinthians 15:19). The writer however, adds more personal reasons.

Ecclesiastes means preacher, or teacher, or philosopher. The author wrote under the *nom de plume* of Solomon, noted both for wealth and wisdom, to say nothing of the pleasures of the flesh. He wrote about 200BC, when Greek culture was spreading everywhere. The terrible suffering brought about by Antiochus had not yet fallen on the country. The suffering of meaninglessness, though less sharp, can be of equal depth.

The book opens with three depressing statements. All is vanity. There is nothing new under the sun. Wisdom only brings vexation and grief (1:1–17).

Finding no joy in wisdom, the preacher turned to sensual pleasure. But a round of riotous parties, flowing with wine and heady laughter, he found to be only a form of madness (2:1–3).

He then turned to creative activity, gardening, home improvement, making money, and going in for culture. Everything he wanted he got. But did it bring happiness or content? No, only weary boredom. He had to admit he'd been acting like many a fool before him (2:15). He came to hate life. His conclusion? All is vanity.

Chapter 3 contains the well-known passage on time. There is a right time for everything, even disillusionment. The following chapters contain proverbs giving advice on how to live with this. Their recipe is moderation in all things. Don't be too righteous or too wicked. In other words, don't screw yourself up to an unauthentic standard of religious and moral behaviour. If you do decide on action, do your best (9:10). For one thing, it gives you more satisfaction. For another, only then will you discover the inevitable truth, that it too is vanity. Make the most of youth, for all too soon, it will pass.

The last chapter contains a moving and poetic description of the approach of old age and death (12:1–7). As mentioned in the introduction the Good News Bible is particularly vivid here. The last verses are a postscript by another hand. Its conclusion is a platitude. Trust God. Keep his commandments. His judgment will be pronounced on our lives. Maybe these verses were added to gain the book's inclusion into the canon of Scripture. The same hand may have added the last three verses of chapter 2. They clothe the preacher's cynical outlook with some rags of pious respectability.

As the Psalmists were honest about their fear and anger, so the preacher is honest about his disillusionment. Sometimes it is only when the point of total despair is reached that God breaks through. It then becomes a door to deeper and truer insight. This is illustrated by the Book of Job.

A drama on the problem of suffering   *Job*

Job is the only drama of the Old Testament. Its theme is the problem of innocent suffering.

The traditional answer was that suffering is a punishment for sin. Sometimes it is, and we bring it on ourselves, as when we abuse our body with alcohol or drugs. Sometimes it is inflicted by others, as when we are smashed up by a drunken driver. The problem may start here, as we ask, 'What have I done to deserve this?' When calamity descends on good people, for no apparent reason, we are bewildered. Sometimes we lose our faith. The preacher in Ecclesiastes rejected the traditional answer, but had no alternative to offer. This is what the author of the Book of Job sets out to do.

In chapters 1 and 2 the scene is set in the court of heaven. Satan here is seen as a servant of God, in the role of accuser. He accuses Job, a good man, blessed with health, wealth and happiness, of being good because it pays him. Similar today is the work of the devil's advocate in the process of canonizing a saint. His task is to show up any possible flaws. God shows his confidence in Job by allowing Satan to test—tempt—Job. A series of calamities deprives Job of his wealth and family. His faith holds, expressed in the wonderful words of 1:21.

Satan is not satisfied. Job himself remains unscathed. God, still trusting Job, permits a further test. Job is struck down by a painful disfiguring disease which causes all to loathe and avoid him. His wife tells him to curse God and die, but Job rebukes her, in further shining words of faith (2:10).

Sitting alone, a tragic figure of suffering, Job is visited by three friends. They hardly recognize him in his disfigurement. For seven days they sit with him in silence. It is the only sensible thing they do. Job at last breaks the silence. He expresses his grief, and curses the day he was born. That prompts his friends to wade in with advice. Each of them has three goes at solving Job's problem, and to each Job makes a reply.

Round 1

Eliphaz starts off with a comforting rebuke. In the past Job has given good advice to those in trouble. Now that trouble has come to him, he has gone to pieces! Eliphaz describes his own terrifying night visions of God's purity which show up man's seeming goodness as sin. Job should accept his suffering in humility and penitence, then, soon, all will be well (chapters 4–5).

Job, naturally, is wanting pity, not empty speeches, from his friends. He insists he has cause for complaint. He does not deserve so heavy a punishment. What evil has he done? His suffering anyhow is pointless. He will continue to complain (chapters 6–7).

Bildad then has his turn. He says life is too short for us to understand such problems. We have to learn from the wisdom of the past. Believe what the fathers have taught. Job answers that if his suffering is God's punishment for sin, it isn't fair that he can't force God to appear in court and give a reason for his judgment. He wants to justify himself, but can't. This leads Job on to accuse God of destroying the good and the bad without distinction (chapters 9–10).

Zophar is shocked into anger. How dare Job accuse God of injustice. Job's claim to be good is bogus. It's a cover-up for a multitude of sins. Even so, if Job repents, all shall yet be well (Chapter 11).

Job retorts with sarcasm. He is fed up with his friends, whom he calls a pack of liars. He turns from them to God, with whom he is determined to argue the matter out to the finish. If his friends think God needs them to defend him they will find themselves rebuked for their temerity. Job's faith mounts to the wonderful climax of 13:15. He will trust God and trust his own integrity, to the point of death.

Round 2
Job 15–21

The arguments of the three friends continue but contain nothing new.

Under pressure, Job's longing to confront God grows (16:21). Again he turns to his friends for pity (19:21). Vain hope! At last there burst from him what is perhaps the most splendid cry of faith in the whole of the Old Testament (19:25– 27). It is also a prophecy of the coming of Christ.

Round 3 Job 22–31

What could the three friends say after that? Nothing apparently. They are stuck in a rut. The old arguments go on being trotted out. Job's longing cry for God touches the heartstrings of our own spiritual search (23:3). But he now believes that God knows the truth about him. His sufferings are a trial out of which his faith will emerge, like gold from the fire. In the light of chapters 1 and 2, Job has reached the truth (23:10).

This is not, however, the end of the drama. Job delves still deeper. There is more to learn. But before the final dénouement there seems to be an interval, a recap. Chapter 28, a hymn to Wisdom, is probably an insertion. In chapter 29 Job recites his good deeds and describes the honour he received from everyone in consequence.

Chapter 30 describes how far from being honoured, he is now shunned and loathed. In chapter 31 he declares that had he, in truth, committed any of the evil deeds which he lists, he would accept God's punishment. So, in part, Job did accept the traditional view. What he was challenging was not the teaching of his friends, but its application. The verdict of guilty, in his case, was unjust.

At this point another character appears on stage. Apparently he had been around all the time listening. Elihu is young and claims that he had kept silent thus far out of respect for his elders. It looks as if these chapters too are a later addition, another effort to uphold tradition and refute Job. If so, it fails. Elihu is wordy. He goes on for six chapters, but has nothing new to say. He rebukes Job and defends God with all the arrogance of youth. His argument is that God is great. To question or challenge him is wicked. Job must shut up.

Then God, out of a whirlwind, interrupts. Job is told to stand up and with wonderful irony, to let God question him! (38:1–3). The poem about God's greatness in creation should be read in the matchless English of the Authorized Version. What seems to be another version of the confrontation follows, after which there is another glorious poem. Job, his smugness flattened, is repentant and silenced (42:1–6). His wish has been granted. God has appeared. But Job has nothing to say.

Has God only done what Elihu tried to do? Evidently not, for God goes on to rebuke the friends and defend Job. He had spoken more truly than they. The whirlwind blew aside the whole system of rewards and punishments doled out to the good and bad, though it took the cross and resurrection to turn the system onto its head. Meanwhile, the friends stand in need of Job's prayers. In the wonderful words of 42:10 Job is healed as he prays for his friends.

The end seems rather an anticlimax. All Job had lost is restored threefold. Don't let this fairy-tale ending conceal what the dramatist has said. Job was given no answer to the problem of suffering. Jesus gave no answer either. Job was given what he was really seeking most, a personal encounter with God. Like Jacob at Penuel, Job had battled with God and prevailed. To know God is to trust him.

For us, the God who waits for us to pierce the shadows concealing his presence is our crucified Lord. He shares our pain, and our pain is a sharing of his. People whose suffering has been transformed by such an experience are bringers of courage and hope to others who are passing through the shadowlands.

A love duet   *The Song of Solomon*

This small gem of a book also nearly got left out of the canon. Books were selected only if they threw light on the relationship between God and his people. This is a love poem full of sensual images. It was included because the Jews saw it as an allegory of the love between God and Israel. The Church has transferred this to the love between Christ and his Church, as well as the individual soul.

The poem is set in the context of Solomon's love for Abishag, the Shunammite girl who looked after King David in his old age. It seems that the young Solomon loved her (1 Kings 1:1–4; 2:19–23; Song of Solomon 3:11; 6:13). Some commentators believe that her real love was not for Solomon but a simple shepherd. The imagery of the poem links the king and the shepherd together.

What can the poem mean for us today? Ecclesiastes and the Book of Job show us that disillusionment can be a path leading us to God. The Song of Solomon shows us that the experience of sexual love can do so too. God is no prude. He created our sexuality with its sensual delight. He made it a means of our sharing in his creativity. All his gifts can be abused, but the inclusion of such a poem in Holy Scripture is a big 'Yes' to the joy of sensual love when blessed by God.

Christians through the ages have found this poem food for contemplative prayer. At its best, our relationship with God is a love duet. We may think this is beyond us, but we may also be surprised to find how much of the imagery of this poem echoes our own experience. Here are a few examples:

> ### *Draw me, we will run after thee.* (1:4)

The soul calls on God to draw her to himself. As passers-by will stop to see what someone is looking at, so does the steady gaze of a loving obedient heart, fixed on God, attract others to join the search. The desired end of contemplative prayer is union of the soul with God, which only God can bring about. He who draws will finally bring the soul into his presence where there is fullness of joy (Psalm 16:11).

He brought me to the banqueting house, and his banner over me was love. (2:4)

These words are now a much-loved chorus. They can be related to the wonder of Holy Communion, but need not be limited to that.

I sleep but my heart waketh. (5:2)

Haven't we all known that experience of God calling us when we are too tired, or too lazy, to respond? When we repent, we find he has gone from us. Then it is we who go desperately searching for him.

It has been said that this love poem describes a game of lovers' hide-and-seek. The one who hides is not afraid of being caught, though there may be a delicious shiver of anticipation. The real point of the hiding lies in the joy of being found. Likewise, for the one who seeks, such hiding only arouses a still greater love and longing to find.

The game is played out in a number of locations, all deeply symbolic: the sheep pastures, the vineyard, the apple orchard, the garden, the banqueting hall, the inner chamber and the mother's house. The deeper we go into prayer, the deeper the meaning we find in the text. The inclusion of the Song of Solomon in the canon of Scripture witnesses to the awesome, glorious truth that our relationship with God is to be a love affair.

The reason for commenting on it at this point is that in times of great disturbance, violence, pain and fear, people turn to prayer.

The fourteenth century was such a time. The Peasants' Revolt and the Black Death damaged and decimated the nation, while the sight of two rival Popes divided and disfigured the Church. Yet this was the age that produced England's greatest mystics—Richard Rolle; the author of *The Cloud of Unknowing*, Walter Hilton and, perhaps most famous of all, Mother Julian of Norwich.

The prosperous and comfortable Church of the eighteenth and nineteenth century neglected their writings. Today we live in another age of turmoil, and these books, republished in paperback, are widely read. More and more people attend retreats, and ask for spiritual direction. There is no longer any need for young people to seek for this in India or Tibet. We have a rich Christian heritage here at home, now restored to us.

A woman who saved her nation   *Esther*

The Book of Job is about the suffering of an individual. Pain led Job to ask questions. The last two books, Esther and Daniel, are about the suffering of a nation, which led both people to courageous sacrificial action.

Esther is yet another book that was included only after much debate. It was written about 300BC. It is the story of a Jewess, chosen by the Persian King Ahasuerus (the Hebrew name for Xerxes), to become his queen, who, by an act of courage, saves her people from massacre. Its position in the Bible is related to its historical context, but there is no outside confirmation of any of the facts the story contains. It does provide, however, an explanation for the origin of the Jewish feast of Purim. It is a dramatic story with a bloody end. Pogroms against Jews have a long history, and it is horrible to see a revival of anti-Semitism in our own time. Partly it is jealousy at their success. This leads to scapegoating. Partly it is because of their refusal to compromise. Mordecai refused to bow to Haman because he refused to bow to anyone but God.

This is made clear in the additions to the story found in the Apocrypha. These include prayers by Mordecai and Esther, and a much more detailed and dramatic description of her appearance before the king.

What are we to learn from the story apart from an increased horror of anti-Semitic violence?

The crisis for Esther comes with Mordecai's letter (4:13–14). It is a call to risk her life to save her nation. It is also a call for her to recognize this as her vocation. It was for this she had been destined to become queen. All through the ages, when things have seemed hopeless for the Church, God has raised up saints who shone as lights in a dark world. In the Bible we see how God raised Joseph, Moses and Gideon. Francis of Assisi, Luther and Wesley were similarly called.

It was in the fullness of time that Jesus was born. The world was fully prepared for the rapid spread of the gospel. There was a universal language, Greek, a universal peace and a good road system, Roman, and the Jewish state was set upon a course that was to lead, in AD70, to its destruction. Had Jesus come fifty years later it would, humanly speaking, have been too late. God's timing is perfect.

Esther leaves us asking, what is the significance of our times for us?

The Book of Daniel

The Book of Daniel was written between 167–164BC, in the period covered by the Books of the Maccabees.

Alexander the Great defeated the Persian Empire in 331BC. After his death, leaving no successor, his empire broke up into three parts—

Egypt, Syria and Greece. Judah eventually became part of Syria, of which, in 175BC, Antiochus Epiphanes became ruler. As we have seen, he set out to force the Jews into the mould of Greek civilization. In 167BC his army entered Jerusalem, pillaged and burnt the city, and knocked down its walls, built with such devotion by Nehemiah. They also desecrated the temple, polluting it with pigs, and raising on the altar site an altar to Zeus—'the abomination of desolation' (Daniel 11:31; compare Matthew 24:15–16). All books of the Law they could find they burnt. Anyone who practised the Law by circumcising children, keeping dietary rules, or observing the sabbath, was put to death. The people were ordered to sacrifice to Greek gods. Many Jews stood firm, and suffered torture and terrible martyrdom. Then Mattathias, a priest, revolted and led a holy war, which, after his death, was carried on by his sons, led by Judas, known as Maccabaeus. Early in the campaign the Jewish forces were attacked on the sabbath, and refused to resist and break the Law. The result was massacre. After this they decided they would have to break it sufficiently to defend themselves. These events are recorded in 1 Maccabees 1–3.

The sufferings of the exile had been accepted as punishment for disobeying the Law. Now God was allowing his people to be massacred for being faithful to it. Psalms 74 and 102 reflect their anguish and bewilderment. The Book of Daniel was written to give them hope.

The writer took the name of a great man from the past round whom to weave his stories. Daniel was one of the princes taken into exile by Nebuchadnezzar.

The first chapter describes how Daniel refused to eat the king's food which would have been offered to idols. This was something the Jews were being forced to do (1 Maccabees 1:62). In chapter 2 Daniel interprets the king's dream. It is an allegory of four empires, Babylonian, Mede, Persian and Greek, which are smashed by a great stone, cut without hands, meaning by God. Here we enter the realm of apocalypse and eschatology, visions of the end. It is a prophecy that points us to Christ.

Chapter 3 tells the story of the burning fiery furnace with its fairy-tale repetitions. But being thrown into furnaces was, to the Jews of the writer's day, no fairy tale (2 Maccabees 7). The splendid faith expressed in Daniel 3:17–18 was both expressed and lived out by them. The mysterious fourth man points us to Christ, who is with us in suffering, as he was, though yet unknown, with those who died for their faith.

Chapter 4 is a warning that pride leads to a fall, even for kings. According to 2 Maccabeus 9:1–13, when Antiochus heard that Jerusalem had been retaken by the Jews, he fell into a melancholy that led to his death, after admitting the evil he had done. A similar death is recorded of Herod Agrippa (Acts 12:21–23). Nebuchadnezzar's boast recalls the story of the tower of Babel. Made godless by self-glory, humans lose their humanity, and power can drive them towards madness. The Greeks called such self-destructive pride *hubris*. It is the theme of the great Greek tragedies.

Such *hubris* is seen again in the story of Belshazzar's feast (chapter 5). Belshazzar was not Nebuchadnezzar's son, and it was Cyrus, not Darius, who took the city. After four hundred years such facts are forgotten. They are not important. What matters is the writing on the wall, an expression we still use today to express nemesis. God, who judged and overthrew Belshazzar, will do the same to Antiochus. So he did. So he has done to other tyrants, as we see all around us today.

The next story shows how the princes, jealous of Daniel's integrity, plot to destroy him through his one point of vulnerability, his religion. No one else cared about the ban on worship, only Daniel. In the second century, Jews were daily courting death by continuing to worship God. Note how courageously public Daniel's worship was.

'Is thy God able to deliver thee?' asks the king. Daniel's answer is a resounding 'Yes'. Psalm 57, probably written at this time, describes the experience of being amidst lions (verse 4). How triumphantly the same faith is expressed.

These stories, secretly told and retold, must have brought strength and hope to people threatened with death. But more was needed, assurance that evil times would end, and God's cause would finally triumph.

Earlier prophets had spoken of a day of the Lord, as an event in history. Later, in more desperate times, it was seen as the last days, an intervention by God at the end of time. This is found in Daniel's vision, described in chapter 7. The four beasts represent the same four empires as before. The little horn is Antiochus, and several verses relate to his war with the Maccabees. The most important verses for us are 13–14. They provide the title Jesus chose to use when referring to himself. He quoted them at his trial (Matthew 26:63–66). It was seen as a messianic claim, and led directly to his death. The 'Ancient of Days' (vv. 9, 13, 22) appears again in John's Vision of Christ, the Alpha and Omega (Revelation 1:13–15). The prophecy of the rule of the saints (Daniel 7:22) also reappears (Revelation 20:4).

Up to this point the Book of Daniel was written in Greek. Now it changes to Hebrew. Daniel's visions, like those of John, become politically dangerous. They are not prophecy, in the sense of foretelling dates, but a coded description of the political events of the time. They become increasingly detailed and accurate as they become increasingly contemporary. A glaring mistake about Antiochus' end dates the book as being written before that time.

What do these last chapters contain of value for us? They have been a happy hunting-ground for groups such as Jehovah's Witnesses, who often knock on our doors, ever ready to discuss the prophecies of Daniel. They are apt to seize on the numbering of years, linked to a prediction which they calculate to prove and predict all kinds of things, much as statistics are used by politicians today!

These last chapters are prophecy in the sense of a powerful foretelling of the force of evil in the world, and an affirmation of our sure hope in what is to come, summed up in the last verse of the book.

Three things are important. One is Daniel's prayer of confession (9:3–9), part of which is included in the Anglican Prayer Book. Another is the development of belief in angels, and their importance as our protectors. The Jews, together with the Persians, came to believe in a hierarchy of angelic beings. Some archangels were named: Gabriel, the messenger (9:21) and Michael, prince of the heavenly host and defender of God's people (10:3; 21:1; compare Revelation 12:7). Raphael, angel of healing, is found in Tobit (Tobit 2:14–18), one of the books of the Apocrypha.

Do we believe in angels? Jesus did. They ministered to him and strengthened him (Matthew 4:11; Luke 22:43). He knew he could call on them for aid (Matthew 26:53). He also spoke of the special protection they gave to children (Matthew 18:10).

Lastly, in Daniel 12:1–3 we get the first explicit and confident assertion of a belief in resurrection, when good and evil men and women will finally receive a just reward.

The book of these visions of the end is sealed (12:4–9). Only the Lamb of God is found worthy to break these seals (Revelation 5:5–7). Our future lies safely in his hands.

This century has seen the deliberate killing of six million Jews, and more Christian martyrs than any other. To them the Book of Daniel has given inspiration. Many Christian martyrs have related personal experiences of angelic protection. They too have died confident, both in resurrection, and in the final victory of Christ and his kingdom.

So, in this last group of Writings, we see the Jews of the second century BC facing their 'shaking of foundations' in ways that we can recognize as our own: with total disillusionment, agonized questioning, deepening spiritual search, courageous witness, and expectant hope of the final coming of Christ, at the end of the age.

For further reading

1 Peter 3:14–18; 4:12–19; Revelation 2:8–10; 7:9–17

For group discussion

1. How can we help those facing disillusionment or pain?

2. What training does your church provide in meditation and prayer? What help would you find most useful?

3. What is your attitude to the end times? What do you say to Jehovah's Witnesses when they come to your door?

For private reflection

1. Do you feel free to argue with God? If not, who, or what, imposes restraint?

2. How can prayer be a lovers' game of hide-and-seek?

3. Is the end of the world for you a source of fear or expectant hope?

Epilogue

About one and a half centuries intervene between the Book of Daniel and the coming of Christ. It was an age of religious decline.

Judas Maccabeus was killed in battle in 160BC, and his youngest brother Jonathan took command of affairs. As a result of a power struggle between Greece, Syria and Egypt, all three bidding for his support, he was able to gain considerable power for himself. He was appointed high priest, ironically enough by the son of Antiochus Epiphanes, who also sent him a crown. Allying in turn with the different powers, Jonathan also made friends with the Romans, whose power was growing.

Judah now had years of peace, freedom of religious observance, and some self-government under a high priest, ruling as king. But power brought corruption. The aristocratic priestly party, the Sadducees, were happy to compromise and collaborate with the Greeks, as they later did with the Romans, in order to keep their power and precarious independence. The ever-changing alliances, and the internal power struggles, disgusted the pious—the strict brotherhood of the Pharisees, who had cared only for the battle of religious freedom. Their militants were the Zealots. In 63BC, the Romans were called in to mediate between the factions. It was the old story of foxes calling in the wolf. The Romans took control, and this was the state of affairs when Jesus was born.

The tension between the secular political parties, and the Orthodox religious parties is very apparent in Israel today. Neither is strong enough to do without the other. A similar tension is seen in Islamic states, such as Iran. The real problem for Israel today is not the threat from her neighbours, but the loss of her sense of final vocation. The one who came to enable her to fulfil it is rejected by both parties.

As we look back on the long history of the Jewish race, we see God working out his plan of salvation.

It starts with the call of one man, Abraham. It branches out, through his descendants, into twelve tribes. These grow to become a nation under their ideal King David. With Solomon, they start looking for political power, becoming like other nations. This in fact was why they originally demanded a king (1 Samuel 8:5). The kingdom split into two, and both turned towards idolatry in order to fulfil their political ambitions. The prophets denounce, warn, proclaim and call to these people in God's name. Though most disregard, a faithful few believe. Both kingdoms are conquered, destroyed and scattered. Then, purified by the exile, a remnant returns to rebuild. No new age dawns, and disillusionment sets in. The faithful remnant dwindles, as power politics again takes over. When Jesus comes, there was only a handful waiting to receive him.

The failure didn't lie just with sin and disobedience. There were different visions of how God was working out his plan. All contained truth, all were flawed, and needed the insight of the others.

There was the Law, with its priestly sacrifices—'images of the true'. Only by blood sacrifice, the release of life, could sinful men and women be cleansed, and brought into a covenant relationship with God. This deep insight was lost, as the sacrificial system degenerated into empty ritual. The prophets, with their moral fervour, attacked this abuse, frequently throwing out the baby with the bath water. The only sacrifice necessary, they declared, was obedience to God, shown in acts of justice and mercy. But the reforms they began were short-lived. Their preaching was not able to create new hearts in people. Something deeper, and more costly, was needed, namely sacrifice.

Then there was the temple, where God's presence was assured. But behind its façade, people were worshipping idols. God deserted his house and let it be destroyed. Yet those who, in exile, discovered his presence with them there, returned with enthusiasm to rebuild the temple. Then again it was destroyed, and yet again.

There were the city walls. What value had they? What dedicated effort was put into their rebuilding! Nehemiah used them to lock the foreigners out. But the three Isaiahs had all seen visions of the Gentiles flocking into the city. Zechariah had said that no wall should act as a constraint. God himself would be a wall of fire around it. Nehemiah and Ezra tried to enforce separation, for experience had shown that mixing with other people led to mixing with their religion. But only by going out to them, as Jonah was forced to do, could they bring God's message of salvation to the world.

Then there was the king and the kingdom, the hope that a Branch, from the root of Jesse, would usher in an age of justice, peace and prosperity. But when the crown was restored by the son of the man who tried to stamp out their religion, it was given to a worldly high priest, by whom politics and power were given top priority.

Finally, there was the problem of suffering. The traditional belief, that the good were rewarded and the evil punished in this life, was contradicted by the experience of those who wrote many of the Psalms, the Book of Ecclesiastes and Job. The servant songs pointed to a strange figure of innocent suffering, bearing the sin of others. Was this an image of the Jewish nation? Were they always innocent? Thousands of Jewish men, women and children died as martyrs to preserve their faith during the persecution of Antiochus Epiphanes, but, when it ended, religion declined into apathy and worldly compromise, or withdrew into narrow legalism, that nourished self-righteousness.

So, the curtain descends upon Act One with the story at an impasse. It is the perfect dramatic moment, when the conflict reaches a crisis, pointing us forward with expectancy to Act Two. This will introduce a new situation, created by the introduction of a new character, a catalyst, who will give the plot a new direction and determine the outcome at the end.

Appendices

Appendix 1

Images of Christ in the Old Testament

Word of God .... Genesis 1:1–3
compare Isaiah 55:8–11
Image of God .... Genesis 1:26
Seed of Eve .... Genesis 3:15
Melchizedek .... Genesis 14:18
Isaac's substitute .... Genesis 22:8
Passover lamb .... Exodus 12:3–13
Bread of heaven .... Exodus 16:21–22
Rock .... Exodus 17:6
Covenant lamb .... Exodus 24:8
Scapegoat .... Leviticus 16:21–22
Brazen serpent .... Numbers 21:8–9
Star of Jacob .... Numbers 24:17
Second Moses .... Deuteronomy 18:15
Second Joshua .... Joshua 1:1–2
Son of David .... 2 Samuel 7:12
Temple of God .... 1 Kings 8:27–29
Redeemer .... Job 19:25
Son of God .... Psalm 2:7–8
compare Daniel 3:25
God's holy one .... Psalm 16:10
Lover and beloved .... Song of Solomon 2:4
Immanuel .... Isaiah 7:14
Prince of Peace .... Isaiah 9:6
Branch of Jesse .... Isaiah 11:1
Saviour .... Isaiah 19:20
Keyholder .... Isaiah 22:22
Cornerstone .... Isaiah 28:16
Way of Holiness .... Isaiah 35:8
Suffering servant .... Isaiah 53
Intercessor .... Isaiah 59:16
Light to Gentiles .... Isaiah 60:1–3
Liberator .... Isaiah 61:1–3
Lord our righteousness .... Jeremiah 23:6
Good shepherd .... Ezekiel 34:23
Son of man .... Daniel 7:13–14
Messiah .... Daniel 9:26

Ruler of Israel..Micah 5:2
King .... Zechariah 9:9
Fountain ....Zechariah 13:1
Messenger of covenant .... Malachi 3:1–3
Sun of righteousness .... Malachi 4:2

Note: there are others

Appendix 2

Quotations and references to the Old Testament made by Jesus according to St Matthew's Gospel

Appendix 3

Genealogy of the tribes

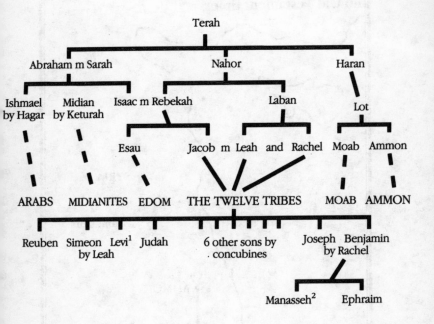

[1] Levi the priestly tribe was landless

[2] Joseph's portion was divided between his two sons or half-tribes

Appendix 4

Israel's neighbours

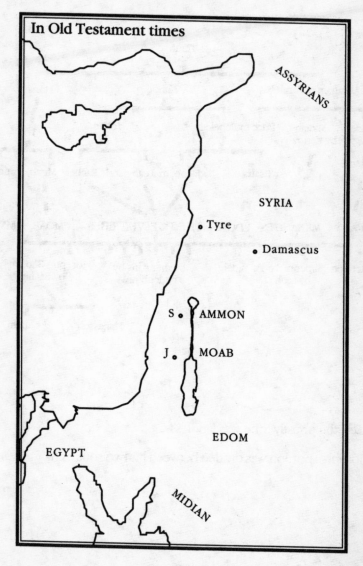

In Old Testament times

ASSYRIANS

SYRIA

Tyre

Damascus

S. AMMON

J. MOAB

EDOM

EGYPT

MIDIAN

Key: S = Samaria
J = Jerusalem

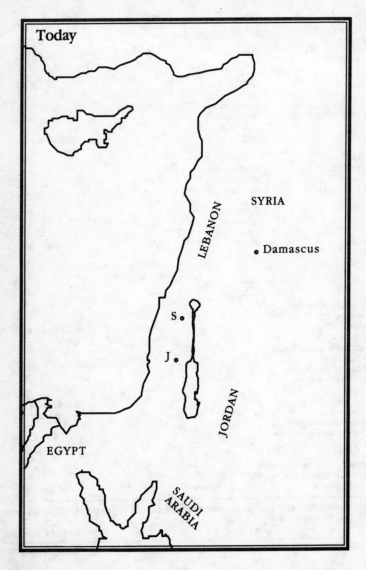

Today

SYRIA

LEBANON

• Damascus

S.

J.

JORDAN

EGYPT

SAUDI
ARABIA

Chronology of the kings

Judah	Israel	Syria	Empires
Rehoboam (17)	Jeroboam		Egypt
Abijam (3)			
Asa (42)	Nadad (2)m	Benhadad I	
	Basha (24)		
	Elah m		
	Zimri (7 days) m		
	Omri (7)		
Jehoshaphat (25) Pact with	Ahab married Jezebel (21) k	Benhadad II m	
Jehoram (19) marries Athaliah	Ahaziah (2) k		
	Joram (12) m		Assyria
Ahaziah m	Jehu (29)		853BC defeats small states
Athaliah (6) m			
Jehoash (37) m	Jehoahaz (17)		
Amaziah (25)	Joash (16)	Hazael	
Azariah (Uzziah) (52)	Jeroboam II		
	Zechariah (6 months) m		
	Shallum (1 month) m		
	Menahem (10)		
	Pekiah (2) m		
Jotham	Pekah m	Rezin	Pul = Tiglath-pileser
Ahaz (16)	Hoshea		
		732BC Damascus falls to Tiglath-pileser	
	722BC Samaria falls to Shalmaneser		
Hezekiah 701BC Jerusalem besieged by Sennacherib			
Manasseh (55)			612BC Nineveh falls to Babylon
Amon (2) m			
Josiah (31) k at battle of Megiddo by Neco of Egypt			
Jehoahez (3 months)deposed and taken to Egypt by Neco			
			605BC Battle of Carchemish Neco defeated by Nebuchadnezzar
Jehoiakim (11)			
Jehoiachin (Conniah) 598BC deported with nobles to Babylon by Nebuchadnezzar			
Zedekiah 587BC blinded and deported; Jerusalem destroyed by Nebuchadnezzar			

Key The numbers in brackets, where given, indicate the length of reign according to the Books of Kings. They do not add up and can't be relied upon.

m = murdered   k = killed in battle